Diamond Key
for Opening the Wisdom Eye

ཤེས་རབ་མིག་འབྱེད་རྡོ་རྗེ་བ་ལམ་གྱི་ལྡེ་མིག།

other books by

Geshe Dakpa Topgyal

Death A Natural Part of Life

Essential Ethics

Holistic Health: A Tibetan Monk's View

The Quest to Safeguard Wholesome Family Life

Refuge

The Tibetan Buddhist Home Altar

Two Subtle Realities: Impermanence and Emptiness

Your Mind, Your Universe

Zuflucht — Buddhistische Zufluchtnahme

DIAMOND KEY
for Opening the
WISDOM EYE

A Guide to the Process of Meditation

Second Edition

Geshe Dakpa Topgyal

Radiant Mind Press
CHARLESTON, SOUTH CAROLINA

Second Edition, 2021

Copyright © 2004–2021 by Geshe Dakpa Topgyal

Cover art © 2021 by Tsering Rabgyal

Photo credits: Cover meditator, Tsering Rabgyal, original art; Pink lotus, jintana, Adobe Stock; Orange marble, Cobalt, Adobe Stock; Candle, v74, Adobe Stock; Buddha, bendao, Adobe Stock; White rose, Dakpa Topgyal, original photo.

All rights reserved. No part of this book may be reproduced in any form or by any means, electronic or mechanical, including photography, recording, or by any information storage and retrieval system or technologies now known or later developed, without permission in writing from the publisher. For permission requests, write to the publisher at the address below.

ISBN 978-1-952518-02-7

Published by Radiant Mind Press
12 Parkwood Avenue
Charleston, South Carolina 29403
geshetopgyalbooks@gmail.com

Acknowledgements

THIS REVISED BOOK WOULD not have been possible without the support of three virtuous friends who I wish to thank deeply and humbly. Our karmic connection brought us together at the right time and place for the purpose of bringing this second edition to reality for the benefit of interested learners.

I start by thanking Ms. Sheila Low-Beer, who collaborated diligently with me on this endeavor. Her generosity of time and energy have made this book clearer, more concise and more accessible to readers.

I respectfully also want to thank Ms. Cynthia Laurrell for her efforts in proof-reading the entire manuscript, helping to refine challenging topics, and formatting the book to prepare it for publication.

Finally, I kindly thank Mr. Tsering Rabgyal, talented artist who trained at the Norbulingka Art Institute in Dharamsala, India. He created the beautiful and inspiring artwork for the book cover and chapter openers.

It is my humble hope that this book will be helpful to all who aspire to know their mind, their life, and the world around them and to realize their highest potential for the benefit of themselves and others.

Geshe Dakpa Topgyal

Dedication

May the merit collected from writing this book implant an enlightened seed in the mind of every reader of this book.

Om Ah Ra Pa Tsa Na Dhi

[Manjushri's mantra of wisdom]

Contents

Foreword 1
Author's Introduction to the Revised Edition 3

Why Meditate? 7
General Nature of the Ordinary Mind 8

What Meditation Is, What Meditation Is Not 19
What Meditation Is 21
Two Basic Types of Meditation 22

Creating Conditions, Choosing Objects 29
Creating Favorable Conditions 29
Objects of Meditation 32

How to Meditate 43
The Nine Stages of Calm Abiding 49
Hindrances to Meditation 56
How to Find the Object of Meditation 57
More on How to Find the Object of Meditation 62

Other Supportive Practices 71
Merit and Purification 71
Physical Health 72
Regarding Food 75
Offerings 76

Ultimate Analysis: "Abiding in the Very Conclusion" 81
Vipassana Meditation 84
Levels of Understanding 85
Impermanence 85
Reasoning for Full Understanding
of Subtle Impermanence 89
Emptiness 94
The Ultimate Analysis 106

The Road Map of the Paths and Bhumis 117
Path of Accumulation 124
Path of Preparation or Linking 125
Path of Seeing and the First Bhumi 126
Path of Meditation and Remaining Nine Bhumis ... 130
Path of No More Learning 144
The Three Kayas 145

Conclusions 147
About the Author 153

༄། ཤེས་རབ་མེད་
འབྱེད་ཚོ་རྗེས་
ལམ་གྱི་སྒྲེ་མེད་།།

Title of the book rendered in Tibetan by Geshe Dakpa Topgyal

༄༅། །དགའ་ལྡན་ཁྲི་ཐོག་བརྒྱ་པ་རྗེ་བཙུན་བློ་བཟང་ཉི་མ།

H. H. The 100th Gaden Tripa Lobsang Nyima

Date ..../......../......

༄༅། །བྱེད་འོན་རྣམ་དཔྱོད་ཞི་བའི་གནས་ཐོབ་ཅིང་། །
ལྷག་མཐོང་རྟོག་པ་ཚོགས་སྟོར་སྐྱེན་ལེགས་པའི། །
མཐོང་ལམ་རྣམ་པར་མི་རྟོག་ཡམ་སྐོམ་པས། །
སྒོམ་ལམ་འབྲས་བུ་མཆོག་གནས་ཐོབ་མོག །

ཅེས་སྐྱོན་པའི་ཚིག་གིས་མདུན་གསུམ་སྟེ་འབྲས་སྦྱོར་གསུམ་གྱི་དགེ་བ་ཞེས་
གསས་པ་སྟོབས་རྒྱལ་མཆོག་ནས་ཆད་ལུས་བཤས་གནེན་དུ་རྩི་བ་ཞབས་དུ་
གཙུག་ཏུ་བཀུར་ཏེ་གཞུར་ཆེན་ལྟུ་ལ་ཐོས་བསམ་སྒོམ་གསུམ་ཡ་མ་བྲལ་བའི་
སྒོ་ནས་གསན་བསམ་རྣམ་པ་བགྱིས་ཏེ་འཆད་ཉེན་ཚོག་གསུམ་གྱིས་བསྐྲུན་
པ་སྐྱིན་པ་དང་སྔགས་པ་ད་ཨམ་ཞི་སྒྲུགས་དང་། ས་བཅུ་ལས་ཐ། འབྲས་བུ་
སྐུ་གསུམ་གྱི་རྣམ་བཞག་བསྟན་པའི་ལེགས་པ་ཆད་བདེ་རྐྱེད་དང་མཐོན་མཐོང་
མོག་གིས་མི་བཅད་པར་གོ་བའི་ཞིང་རྣམས་འགྱུར་ཕྱུན་སུམ་ཚོགས་པའི་
ལ་བསྒགས་པ་དང་། བསྟན་པ་རྒྱས་པའི་རྒྱུ་དུ་འགྱུར་བའི་སྨོན་འདུན་བཅས་
དགའ་ལྡན་ཁྲི་ཐོག་བརྒྱ་པ་བློ་བཟང་ཉི་མས་སྨྲ་ཆེས་བཟང་པོའ།། །

Drepung Loseling Tsawa Khangtsen, P.O.Tibetan Colony - 581 411, MUNDGOD. Distt : Karwar (K. S.) INDIA

Foreword

May one reach the Path of Accumulation and the Path of Linking
Through full insight realization
Which is achieved upon the perfection of Shamatha
By overcoming laxity and pacifying discursive thoughts.
May the ultimate level of attainment be achieved
As a result of the cultivation of the Path of Seeing
And the Path of Meditation (direct, non conceptual realization).

With the above aspirational prayers I introduce Geshe Dakpa Topgyal of Drepung Loseling, Dakpa Khamtsen, who has studied with extreme devotion the five major Buddhist philosophies from various great masters by embracing listening, contemplation, and meditation.

He is most qualified to teach and perpetuate the Buddha Dharma through giving teachings and writing.

I highly recommend this book on Shamatha and Vipassana meditation, the Five Paths and Ten Bhumis, and the Fruition of the Three Kayas, which are presented in depth, free from obsolete expressions, and enriched with his personal experiences, thus making them easy to understand. May this book become the cause for the flourishing of the Buddha Dharma.

The 100th Gaden Tripa Lobsang Nyima
February 12, 2004

Author's Introduction to the Revised Edition

IN THE SEVENTEEN YEARS since *Diamond Key for Opening the Wisdom Eye* was first published, the number of publications related to meditation and mindfulness has skyrocketed. As the practice of meditation has grown, more people may be experiencing its benefits, but there is also a risk of watering down and distorting the Buddha's authentic teachings on the subject. This makes the original purpose of the book even more relevant today. Extensively revised, this second edition includes color photos to illustrate various concepts and objects of meditation, further clarifies difficult passages, and provides additional information.

The subject of this book is meditation as well as the Five Paths and Ten Bhumis. The Five Paths and Ten Bhumis are the complete spiritual road map for the attainment of Nirvana or liberation and Enlightenment or omniscience. The ultimate result of training in meditation is to lay the groundwork for the journey through the sequential order of the Five Paths and Ten Bhumis.

My intention and purpose in writing this book is to make a clear distinction between what meditation is and what meditation is not, and furthermore to present a clear understanding and proper method of Tibetan Mahayana Buddhist meditation. With this I hope to remove many of the preconceived ideas about Buddhist meditation, which in its authentic form remains a fairly new concept and practice within the Western world and its culture.

At the same time, in conjunction with the presentation on Vipassana meditation, this book clearly explains the Buddhist concepts of subtle impermanence and emptiness, which are beyond the understanding or comprehension of the untrained, ordinary human mind.

The presentations on subtle impermanence and emptiness are based on the flawless teachings of the great third and fourth century Indian masters Nagarjuna, Chandrakirti, and Dharmakirti. These masters' teachings on subtle impermanence and emptiness are considered the most logically and scientifically accurate within Buddhist tradition.

Within Buddhism, Nagarjuna's understanding of emptiness, and Dharmakirti's understanding of the natural law of causality and the law of that-which-is-produced being naturally impermanent, are considered to be the highest and most profound understandings of reality.

With this the reader is invited to take a journey to the heart of mind and walk down the path of Enlightenment for the benefit of self and others.

Geshe Dakpa Topgyal
October 2020

“ Meditation is an inner tool to discover your mind, your life, and the world around you. ”

1

Why Meditate?

THERE IS MORE TO do with your human life than simply struggle for your day to day survival, which, by nature, is a very animal like way of existence, not at all the way a human being should live. You should not alternate your life just between work and worry. What is meant by there being more to do with your human life? It means that you should strive to realize your human potential, the most precious gift of human birth. You should strive to reach a higher spiritual evolution moving towards Enlightenment. You must live an ethical life and cultivate a meditational mind of wisdom realizing the reality of ultimate truth. Take these goals as your road map rather than relying on your own version of truth that you created, not knowing who you really are and what your potential truly is.

If you let yourself alternate between your busy life of work and worry while living in this human form, then you are misusing your human birth/life and only creating the intense causes of the existence of this intense life of samsara. Living this type of life would rob you of a precious opportunity.

Buddhism teaches the ways and means to realize your human potential without needing to live with a restrictive belief in something that you personally don't know about. One of the means that Buddhism teaches is meditation. Meditation is an inner tool to discover your mind, your life, and the world around you. The harshness of the world and the painful experiences of your life (running after something or running away from something) are all caused by your mind failing to recognize its own creation, which is based on delusions, fantasies, confusion, and the mind-luring appearances of external objects.

Meditation is not a way or means to run away from the harshness of the world around you; rather, it is a way to see that the harshness of the world around you is created by your own mind. Meditation gives you the ability to stop your mind from making such a thorny world out of your external environment.

During your meditation sessions you should not be like a rabbit going to his hole to sleep or avoid danger that you don't want to be confronted with. Going into meditation should not be a means to avoid family problems that you would rather not deal with.

In order for you to experience a happy life as well as a happy death it is necessary to understand the following:

- how the mind functions;
- what the mind creates;
- how the mind projects its creation onto the world around you;
- how these projected illusions of the world become real to you;
- how this false belief in them as real develops into a painful emotional response of wanting and not wanting, liking and disliking; and finally,
- how these types of emotions you live with interfere with your relationship with the rest of the world.

General Nature of the Ordinary Mind

How the Mind Functions

Your present mind is functioning on the basis of the active workings of your five senses and the sensory information they get from the world around you and from your own body. Your present mind's knowing capability is very limited and restricted to your five senses. The mind's unlimited and unrestricted knowing capacity is currently numbed, overwhelmed, and obscured by the density of thoughts, emotions, concepts, and ideas. As long as thoughts and emotions are in you, your mind's knowing capability remains at the conceptual level with a limited, restricted, and selective search for something with constant rejection. In brief, your present mind is functioning under the dictations of delusions and latent habituation of seeing things in the way they appear to you or in the way they present themselves to you without room for questioning their validity. Your mind chases after your thoughts and acts accordingly.

Your present mind is constantly doing three things: 1) living too far in your past life experiences and often being too elated or being too depressed; 2) living too far in your future with hope, expectation, anticipation, fear, and the like; 3) constantly engaging in the thinking process, wanting to change your present situation due to seeing something as not quite right, even in your physical environment. For example, the placement of your furniture or paintings in the living room, the color of your bedroom walls, or the condition of your kitchen sink.

There is never a time when your mind rests in mere awareness without constantly doing one of those three. The reason why your mind is constantly thinking is because your mind is looking for full satisfaction. Your mind will stop thinking when it experiences full inner satisfaction arising from within you and not from external sensory objects. In general, your mind tends to think less about something when your mind is somehow happy and content with it. On the other hand your mind tends to think more about something when your mind is discontented. So, it is clear that the reason why your mind is constantly thinking is because it is not content, and therefore searching for satisfaction.

How and What the Mind Creates

The ordinary mind creates a quality of inherence, which does not exist as part of an object's reality. Here inherence means a mode of something being capable to exist as, for example, a "table," without depending on something other than the table itself. You think that "table-ness" or being a table has somehow already existed before you named an object a table due to your need of it as a table. This independent mode of being of the object is called "inherent."

In reality, nothing exists as a table with the mode of being inherent. You only named it a table due to your need of it as a table. When your need of the object as a table is no longer there then the object no longer exists as a table for you.

However, the name "table" does not inject any new quality into that object. But that object now exists as a table because of the name "table," connecting your need of the table with that particular object. The object itself does not have any physical characteristics that designate it as a table, and it is the name "table" bestowed upon it for a user's needs that empowers the object to be a table.

The object does not exist as a table or as non-table before the connection of the name "table" with that object, which is only due to your need of the object as a table.

How the Mind Projects Its Creation Onto the World Around It

The mind projects its creation, such as the quality of inherent attractiveness, through the process of seeing it or taking it as a part of the actual object and thus failing to see that it is coming from your own mind. You value the object, which seems to have the inherent quality of attractiveness or devalue the object, which seems to have the inherent quality of unattractiveness.

Because of the projection, everyone makes up his or her own story about the object, or the person, that is the object of either attachment or repulsion.

The projections of mind corrupt external objects and events. In reality there is no immoral quality (and there is no "moral" quality either) within the object. Immorality is within your own mind. Delusions, distortions, and fantasies in your mind are the immorality in your mind. Your immorally corrupted mind projects immoral qualities onto the object.

For example, there is no immoral quality within alcohol itself. But your desirous mind makes it immoral, something to be avoided with the sense of it as negative immoral consumption. The same applies to sex. There is no immoral quality within sex. But again your desirous mind and lustful thoughts make it immoral by overindulgence and misuse.

All the problems related to alcohol and sex such as addiction, crime, mindless and harmful actions, a dysfunctional family, painful divorce, and so forth come from your corrupted, immoral mind and surely not from the substances or acts themselves. Sex and alcohol can be medicine when they are utilized by a highly disciplined, uncorrupted mind. However, sex and alcohol are things to be avoided in certain restricted religious practices for different reasons and purposes, not because they themselves are negative and immoral.

In general, not only sex and alcohol, but every type of overconsumption and over-indulgence, has its own unhealthy and destructive effects on the consumer. Take for example food. Overconsumption of food creates health problems. This is not because of negativity or immorality within the food. It is solely the problem of your own craving and desirous mind for eating more than what your body really needs. You often forget the purpose of eating, which is just to sustain your material body, which is dependent on gross food. But you often eat to gratify your craving and desirous mind, not to sustain your body. Eating and doing anything that goes beyond the purpose of that thing is naturally unhealthy and destructive to yourself or to others. The root problem of all this is nothing other than your own immorally corrupted mind.

Every part of life that goes beyond what it is meant by nature to be is unhealthy and destructive because of the corrupted mind.

The purpose of drinking alcohol is not to get drunk and then to reveal the faults and imperfections that you really don't want to reveal when you are not drunk. You don't want to show them, in general, for the sake of your own dignity.

The purpose of drinking is just to enjoy the pleasure of it, well before you get drunk. There is no pleasure of drinking wine, for example, when you are totally drunk. The real pleasure of drinking comes from your clear and consciously controlled awareness of the fact that what you are drinking is intended for pleasure and not as a means for you to become irresponsibly drunk.

So, all pleasure in what you do arises only when you are fully aware of the action, agent, and the object that complete the event fully. Full awareness of all three—action, agent, and object—within a shared moment, occurs only due to meditative experience. That experience is actually functioning in post-meditative life, such as eating, taking a shower, and other activities of daily life.

How the Projected Illusions of the World Become Real to You

These illusions become very real to you by serving as the prime source of emotions such as attachment and aversion, liking and disliking, etc. You are trapped in the chain of liking and disliking, wanting and not wanting, greedily running after or fearfully running away. You will never be free from this painful chain of meaningless emotions unless you meditate and gain insight into how your mind works.

The mentally projected value upon an object of attractiveness or unattractiveness becomes real to you when it returns back to you mixed with the object's appearance. Since this quality is not a part of the actual object, it will never match what the object seems to be capable of providing you. Because of this mismatch, your life will be full of disappointment, frustration, and confusion unless you gain insight through meditation. That is why meditation is necessary. Meditating once in a day can make a big difference in your life.

How This False Belief in the Mental Projection as Real Gives Rise to Confusion and Emotional Pain

When the mentally projected value of an object returns to you as real, with the potential to make you happy, you then become attached to the object through seeing your happiness residing somewhere within it. The way you become attached to it is through emotional intimacy with a fear of losing it. When another object's projected value comes back to you as real with the potential of making you unhappy, you are then repulsed by the object, seeing your unhappiness within it. Your repulsion is so strong that you have a wish to destroy the object, ridding your surroundings of it, banishing it from your sight. In both cases, you become attached to or repulsed by your own mental creations.

How Baseless Emotions Interfere in Your Natural Relationship with the World Around You

The emotions of attachment and aversion, wanting and not wanting, liking and disliking are very biased, obsessive, and discriminative in their nature. They narrow your mind and limit your capability to be free and from having an easygoing life without mental and physical barriers and limitations.

They stop you from seeing the truth of reality. They stop you from making direct contact with reality. They bring fear of finding that what you think of as truth is actually untrue. They interfere by preventing you from accepting truth as truth, and untruth as untruth. Your relationship with the rest of the world becomes filled with painful experiences of being rejected, alienated, excluded, trapped, captured and tossed about without a choice.

All of these emotions are created by your own mind and not by the world around you. You will not be free from their negative effects until you tame your mind. Your mind is intoxicated by delusions and fantasies. Delusion does not mean a breakdown of reality, but instead is a misperception of reality.

Seeing things the way you normally think of them is not seeing what they really are. For example, normally you might see some object or person as if they are fully capable of making you happy or with an inherent quality of making you happy. This then leads you to become attached to them, with the hope of them making you happy. But in reality, nothing is inherently capable of making you happy or making you unhappy. Their ability to make you happy, as well as how you will experience them (in a painful or pleasing way) depends solely on your state of mind. If you are looking to the object or person with a positive attitude or calm mind, then that object or person appears to your mind as positive, pleasant, and appealing. If you are looking to the object or person with a negative attitude or disturbed state of mind, then they appear to your mind as negative, unappealing, and hostile. So, how the world around you appears to your mind, as being positive or negative, is solely dependent on your state of mind and attitude.

During your lifetime you have built up a strong habit of relating to things either by greedily running after what you think is good and attractive, or fearfully running away from what you think is bad and unpleasant. This habit of running after and running away is to be expected at the time of death, which will put you in a confused, fearful, and terrifying world of your mental projections.

A calm and peaceful state of mind at the time of death, is extremely important. Your state of mind at the time of death determines the outcome of your rebirth as well as its conditions. A positive state of mind at the time of death activates your positive karma, helping you to be born in a higher rebirth in an environment conducive to spiritual realization. The negative and confused state of mind at the time of death not only causes a painful death, but it activates your negative karma, thus causing you to be born in a lower form with an undesirable environment. So, learning how to die in a peaceful state of mind is very important. If you don't know how to die in peace it is a clear sign of your not knowing how to live in a meaningful way. In other words, if you don't know how to die, then you don't know how to live, because death is a part of your real life.

“ Strive for perfecting Shamatha in the first place if you are honestly aiming to perfect the Vipassana that eradicates all of your delusions from their root. ”

2

What Meditation Is, What Meditation Is Not

THROUGH MEDITATION YOU CAN come to recognize illusions as illusions, fantasies as fantasies and projections as projections, rather than being misled by those forces and trapped under their control. As a result you are able to die with a calm and peaceful state of mind, resulting in a fortunate rebirth in a desirable environment.

Time spent in meditation is not a form of selfish time, in which you enjoy your life in a blank state while bringing nothing in your field of awareness, nor is it a time when you cut all of your normal emotional ties with the world around you.

Temporarily blanking out your mind helps you find temporary relaxation/rest, but this will not help you to return to your daily life activities with a new or fresh awareness, which will prevent you from falling victim to your own mental projections and fantasies. Merely blanking out your mind is not meditation.

Having this type of temporary blank mind is like a metal key being in a metal lock, without opening the door for you to get in. Meditation is like a key to open the door to see things as they really are, beyond the concepts and limitations imposed by your dualistic conceptual mind. You being in that blank state of mind is like a metal key simply resting in a metal lock without opening the door. In this example, you are unable to see what you are looking for, and where you are trying to reach, even though you're in the right place. You are not reaching anywhere. You are doing nothing other than just being in a blank mind, no matter how long you try to be within that state. You will probably rot in there the same way a metal key that has been in the metal lock for a long time gets rusted. Nothing significant will ever be revealed by being in a mere blank or numbed state of mind, no matter how long and how hard you try it.

Simply sitting by yourself with a motionless body is not meditation unless your mind has generated a non-thinking awareness state. When your mind has generated a non-thinking awareness state, you are aware of what is happening in your surroundings in terms of sound, motion, and smell, and other sensory input. But they do not evoke emotion in you and you do not play with them or follow/chase them. You are just you and they are just themselves. When you come out of the meditation, you will find them to be soft and gentle rather than harsh and thorny with an agitating nature. Here you are meditating and enjoying the results of meditation in your post-meditative life.

If you just sit by yourself with a motionless body without generating a non-thinking awareness of mind, only numbing your mind, this will only cause you to find your surroundings more annoying, harsh, and thorny with an agitating nature upon return to your daily activities. Here you are not meditating.

Simply letting your mind fly up in the air is not meditation. Sitting in an absent-minded state is also not meditation. Simply allowing your mind to take you to some exotic internal place, not knowing where you are, why you are there, and how you got there, though you are free from the extremes of feeling happy or unhappy, is also not meditation.

When you are meditating your mind should not be the one to take you somewhere out of your control. Rather you should be the one to decide where your mind will go, where your mind will rest, and what specific thing your mind should be aware of. This is different from the way the non-meditative conceptual mind usually is aware of something during the post-meditation period.

So what is meditation then?

What Meditation Is

Meditation is an inner spiritual discipline to gain full control over your thoughts, emotions, and mind, which means meditation is a process of bringing your thoughts and emotions under your control and not letting them dictate your life. When thoughts and emotions come under your control, then the actions of your body, speech and mind are under your control, and then your life is under your control. As a result, you are free from greedily running after something and fearfully running away from something. Running away from and running after things prevents you from ever getting rest in your life, and this is the real problem that lies within you and for which there is no external cure.

Meditation creates a conducive atmosphere within your emotional or psychological state from which inner peace and wellbeing can arise. This makes you less dependent on external circumstances for your happiness and satisfaction.

There is no meditation that does not bring you a new and fresh awareness, helping you to solve your old problems and preventing new problems from occurring. So, if you are sincerely looking for help then get help from the meditation, the single cure for your life's problems.

Meditation was taught by the Buddha as a single tool or means to attain higher human perception and spiritual realization beyond what is usually achievable by the ordinary human mind. However, you can use meditation for different purposes too. You can use meditation to:

1. Reduce stress.
2. Increase relaxation.
3. Bring your sense of being into a comfortable state and enter into sound sleep to get maximum rest.
4. Release tension in your muscles and nervous system.
5. Release bad *prana*/wind/air or any other negative energies from your body that are created by your negative emotions such as anger, fear, worry, sadness, depression. Negative thoughts and emotions

not only agitate and provoke your mind and its capability to act in a peaceful way, but all the organs in your body also feel in some way very "perplexed" and "depressed." The natural flow of energy, including the blood and air circulation, is disrupted.

6. Clear your mind from congested thoughts and emotions so that you can think well, sleep better, rest better, and remember better.

Two Basic Types of Meditation

In general there are two types of meditation, *Shamatha* and *Vipassana* (Sanskrit). All traditional or authentic techniques of meditation should fall under one of those two categories. Further, we can classify each of those two in terms of objective awareness and subjective experience. Objective awareness means if you are meditating on a tulip flower the undistracted, peaceful attentive mind is simply aware of the fresh image of the tulip. Subjective experience means, for example if you are meditating on compassion, the meditator generates the active feeling of compassion within his or her mind and then sustains the uninterrupted continuity of that feeling of compassion rather than using the compassion as something to be aware of, unlike the tulip flower. Compassion is something to experience rather than something that is simply an object of awareness. Through familiarity, gradually the compassion becomes a refined quality of your mind, unlike the tulip.

In the cultivation of meditation with objective clarity, you simply allow the focal object/observed object to appear in the field of your awareness, making no room within your mind for something else to appear other than the thing that is being purposely designated to be there in your awareness. The designated object could be, for example, an image of Buddha, a rose, or a mantric syllable. You bring the object to your awareness and then simply hold it in the field of your awareness without conceptualizing about it. Without conceptualizing means not simply not thinking about it, but conceptually not adding anything onto it or subtracting anything from it. Just let it be. The very cultivation of this continuity of your awareness of the observed object with a degree of clarity held for a longer period of time is known as meditation with objective clarity.

In the practice of meditation with subjective awareness, you are trying to generate/transform your whole state of mind into the entity of a particular type of consciousness or perception such as love, compassion, or Bodhicitta. Take, for example, meditation on compassion. When you are meditating on compassion, you are trying to generate/transform your whole state of mind into a "pure unselfish wish" for others to be free from suffering and the causes of suffering. And then you simply maintain this "wish" for a longer period of time, let's say fifteen to twenty minutes, without the interference of your concern about your own wellbeing and interests. Usually, your selfish mind is looking out for your own interests even if it means that you are allowing others to suffer a loss. The eight primary worldly concerns that preoccupy you are: mundane gain and loss, happiness and sorrow, praise and blame, fame and infamy.

Meditation on compassion, love, and Bodhicitta belongs to the practice of cultivation of subjective awareness. In this type of meditation, you are not using compassion and love as a focal object for your mind to rest on. Rather your whole state of mind transforms into the entity of compassion and love.

Shamatha and Vipassana meditations are included within the above mentioned two ways of meditation. Any state of mind that is established as a meditation due to its quality of perfect stabilization arising from the sole effort of focusing or concentrating belongs to Shamatha meditation. Any state of mind that is established as meditation due to its quality of employing unique analysis that helps your mind reach beyond the conceptual apprehension or ascertainment of the apprehended object is considered to be Vipassana meditation. How long you can sustain the full force of ascertainment of the object when you have reached beyond the conceptual ascertainment purely depends on the perfection of Shamatha. It is impossible for you to be able to sustain it if you don't have a personal experience of true Shamatha in the first place. Because of this reason Shamatha is said to be the single foundation of all other forms of meditation. The fruitful practice of Vipassana will not occur until you have a really good personal experience of Shamatha.

Therefore, the great Indian master Acharya Asanga said: "... you should strive for perfecting the Shamatha in the first place if you are honestly aiming to perfect the Vipassana that eradicates all of your delusions from their root."

Shamatha Meditation

What is Shamatha? The word Shamatha in Sanskrit means calm abiding. Calm abiding, single pointed, inner silencing, tranquil abiding, and absorption are in many ways interchangeable. But it is important to see the main context of the subject matter. In the context of the subject matter of Shamatha, they are pretty much the same and have the same meaning.

Shamatha is the cultivation of your mind into a state of mere awareness and the mode of resting your mind in that awareness state with total absence of thoughts, emotions, concepts, and ideas for a certain period of time.

Your mind, in this purposely generated state of mere awareness, has full capability of knowing or detecting anything that arises in its awareness that it may not actually know during that actual resting period, in that meditative state of mere awareness. A mind that has the capability to know does not necessarily take the action to know. Doing so would give rise to thought. This is because, until the cultivation of Shamatha when the mode of resting in the entity of mere awareness reaches a certain stage, as soon as the sense of knowing occurs that knowing gives rise to a thought. One single act of actually knowing creates a thought of the thing that is being known. However, if you know something do you really need another thought to confirm it? No. But we have thought after thought. To repeat: Until the meditator reaches a certain level, one single act of actually knowing creates a thought of the thing that is being known, such as the thought of a label or name, or of a judgment that the object is good or bad. This inevitable thought prevents a true apprehension of the object, because it distorts the reality, distorts the fact of what the object really is. The object really is neither more than a name nor merely a name. For example, the mind designates or labels an object as cup or table. An object is a cup or table just because the mind designates it as such. There is nothing in the cup or table to require that it be a cup or table. Objects exist as such and such because of designation. Designation is the thought that arises right after the act of mere knowing.

Vipassana Meditation

What is Vipassana? The word Vipassana in Sanskrit means analytic. The term analytic, special seeing, extra seeing, reaching beyond, seeing beyond, and penetrative are in many ways interchangeable. But again it is important to see the main context of the subject matter. In the context of Vipassana, they are pretty much the same and give the same meaning.

Vipassana is the cultivation of employing subtle analysis within the calm frame of mind of Shamatha. This, as a result, helps you to gain a deep insight into the true nature of reality of all existing phenomena, the insight that you otherwise miss due to your dualistic mind.

“ You should strictly emphasize the quality of the meditation rather than the length of time. ”

3

Creating Conditions, Choosing Objects

Creating Favorable Conditions

How you prepare for meditation and the favorable conditions that you create will impact your progress in meditation. Paying attention to what we wear, the time and place for meditation, our posture and the length of time that we sit are important considerations.

Choice of Clothing

Any loose and comfortable clothing can be worn. The clothing made from natural fabric like cotton and wool is better. Tight shirts, pants and skirts are surely not comfortable and are not good for the energy circulation in your body, including the blood and *prana*. I have noticed that people often wear very tight pants and skirts when they are meditating. Their feelings of discomfort sitting in these clothes shows from their facial expressions after just a few minutes.

The Best Times to Meditate

The best times to meditate are early in the morning before sunrise and in the late afternoon a little before the sun sets. The reason for this is because of the three types of freshness:

1. Freshness of the time
2. Freshness of the body
3. Freshness of the mind

Especially early in the morning is the best time. Your mind is really fresh and has not yet started its thinking process. Your mind is free of tiredness from thinking and from congested thoughts and emotions from that day. If those two times are not suited to your daily activities and responsibilities, then you can meditate at any part of the day whenever there is a free time for your personal use. In any case, meditating on a regular basis is extremely important in order to gain the real benefits of meditation other than temporary relaxation.

Conducive Place to Meditate

If possible, the place where you meditate should have been blessed by a Guru or teacher. It should be quiet and free of dog barking at night and free of human activity. It should be clean, free of dust, mold or mildew. The light should be neither too dim nor too bright, since dim light invites sleepiness and bright light excites the mind. It is good to have some adjustable light so you can alter the light according to your need at that time. The room temperature should be neither too cold nor too hot. In that room there should be no distracting things and objects.

The things to keep in that room are inspiring images, sacred texts, any objects that are more calming and pleasing to your mind. In the modern days all these conditions may be difficult to meet with, but still one should strive for your meditation place to have fifty percent of these qualities suggested by the Buddha and many of the past great yogis and masters.

How to Sit, Your Posture

You can sit in a relaxed and comfortable position. In general, there are eight traditional meditation postures instructed by the Buddha in his Tantric teachings. They are:

Sit in a full lotus posture or cross legged position.

1. Place your hand in the position of meditative equipoise, the left hand beneath the right and the thumbs touching gently to form a triangle. Then let them rest at four inches below the navel.
2. The back or spine should be perfectly straight and upright without being supported.
3. Bend your neck down slightly by bringing your chin towards the chest.
4. Keep your shoulders perfectly even like a flying eagle's wings.
5. The eyes should be slightly open and gazing in a relaxed way somewhere towards the tip of your nose. Or focus gently on the floor about four inches in front of you if this seems more natural.
6. Keep the jaws and lips in a soft and natural state.
7. The tongue should rest gently against the palate just behind the teeth.

Each one of these eight postures has a significant and positive effect on your meditation. However, if you find difficulty sitting with those traditional postures, then you should choose to sit in the most comfortable position. Let your body be very relaxed and naturally free from tension and discomfort. Keeping the spine perfectly straight and upright is mandatory.

How Long to Meditate in One Sitting Session

In the beginning you should not meditate longer than ten to fifteen minutes. You should strictly emphasize the quality of the meditation rather than the length of time.

Increase the time by five minutes only when your meditation has noticeably improved. Whenever you see a need to increase the time of meditation, you should do so by increasing only another five minutes for each time.

Objects of Meditation

In general, an object of meditation is fixed, restricted and limited to certain objects. You have complete liberty to choose the object of your meditation. However, there are certain objects that are more advisable for different reasons and purposes—such as an image of a Buddha, your root Guru, seed letters, pin pointed bright lights, a skeleton covered ground, the breath, chakras, or an internally generated sound. I know that many people like to choose something of external natural beauty such as a flower, a waterfall, or a sun setting over the ocean as an object of their meditation. Those are perfectly fine. The object of meditation is unimportant. What is really important is the cultivation of meditation that has real qualities of either Shamatha or Vipassana.

What is Meant by the Object of Meditation

An object of meditation is an object upon which your mind can relax or rest without thinking, simply being present in the intense awareness of it without attaching or detaching from it. In other words, object of meditation means that which is being observed or watched by your nonthinking mind without emotionally engaging with it.

An object of meditation is a mere mental image or picture of the actual physical object, let's say, an image of the Buddha on a Tibetan thangkha painting or a rose—one that is created, constructed, or conjured by your mind, and then held as real without distinguishing real from unreal and unreal from real. You are not using the actual Buddha's thangkha painting or a rose in front of you by looking at it directly with your eyes. This is not what the "object of meditation" means. Instead, you are using the mentally conjured image of the Buddha or a flower as the single object to be observed or watched by your mind without using actual visual sense perception.

The object of Shamatha meditation is called the "unanalyzed object," whereas the object of Vipassana is called the "analyzed object." This is because in the cultivation of Shamatha, you are not analyzing the object. Rather, you are resting your awareness upon it without conceptualizing. In the cultivation of Vipassana, you are analyzing the nature of the object while your mind is resting on it without the interference of your ordinary concepts of what that object is, how it functions, how it should be, and so forth.

However, the objects of Shamatha and Vipassana need not be different or contradictory to one another. One object can be the object of both Shamatha and Vipassana.

In the beginning you can try various objects and see which one is most suited to your meditation. Once you have found the one that is most effective, then you must keep it as a permanent object of your meditation. You should not change to other objects until you fully attain Shamatha.

The habit of changing the object of meditation very often is a serious mistake in the cultivation of Shamatha and Vipassana meditation. You must not build this habit from the beginning if you are seriously hoping to attain Shamatha in your lifetime.

Choosing Your Object of Meditation

Anything can be used as an object of meditation. However, it can be highly beneficial to select as the object for your meditation a particular object that is more appropriate and feasible for your need, inclination and comfort. For example, in the case of using a flower as your object of meditation, among all possible flowers you may have one personal favorite flower that is more soothing, calming and relaxing to you, such as the pinkish lotus pictured here.

With the serious intention to sit and meditate, leave everything aside, with no obligations to do anything else other than sit and meditate for a period of twenty to thirty minutes (or less or more depending on your time, energy and ability). Let's say for example your object of meditation is this pinkish lotus. Relax your mind, and prevent your mind from thinking while letting go thoughts and emotions as much as you can. At the same time be determined not to welcome any thoughts and emotions that may arise. Thoughts and emotions may arise like clouds in the sky. The clouds move through and dissipate without disturbing the clarity of the sky. Thoughts and emotions can move through and dissipate without disturbing the clarity of the mind. Gradually let your relaxed mind capture the pinkish lotus. Imagine that pinkish lotus is newly bloomed, is extremely fresh and fragrant, captivating, relaxing and comforting for your mind to witness. The pinkish lotus has eighteen petals around the center stamens and pistil.

You may imagine that the pinkish flower is in front of you or that it has grown and bloomed in your own mind. This is up to the individual. In either case concentrate on that pinkish flower, which is your object of meditation, without thinking, conceptualizing and judging. Merely concentrate and observe, witness the flower.

When the mind becomes concentrated on it with one hundred percent of the mind's attention directed on that pinkish flower, then that concentrated mind cannot have room to do anything else except witness that flower as the sole object of its attention. This concentrated mind is in meditation, is itself meditation.

Now, this concentrated state of mind must be supported and guarded by mindfulness and vigilance. If not supported and guarded by these two, you may not be able to sustain concentration for more than a split second. Mindfulness actually prevents the concentrated state of mind from forgetting what it is attempting to do. Mindfulness assists the concentrated state of mind not to lose the concentration quickly and frequently. Vigilance oversees the quality of the concentrated state of mind and detects the errors or pitfalls of meditation such as sleepiness, ideation, excitement, elation or numbness that damage and degrade the quality of the meditation. The qualities of meditation are: full force of concentration, stability, stillness, clarity, freshness, alertness and awareness (not just awakeness). Sleepiness and other hindrances damage the concentration and degrade the concentration leaving it open to random thoughts, concepts, memories.

While the mind is concentrating on that pinkish flower, over time its color may change, its shape may change, or its number may change. Once any of these occur, do not chase after the change, but immediately force the flower to return to its original state.

Mindfulness, vigilance, and this highly concentrated state of mind have to go together and work together, not only to sustain the unbroken continuity of the concentrated state of mind for an extended period of time but also to make consistent progress in meditation, each time you sit and meditate.

When the time comes to discontinue the meditation you should not act like you are waking up from a deep sleep. Rather you should consciously and intentionally or deliberately dissolve that pinkish lotus flower in its emptiness with a sense of appreciation and gratitude that it has served as your object of concentration, that it has let your mind to rest peacefully on it.

Soon after coming out of your meditation, without bringing any thought, let yourself watch your own state of mind and your own state of being and how you really felt when you were in meditation. And then, make sure to take that quality and feeling to the rest of the day.

Creating Conditions, Choosing Objects

If you choose an orange glass marble or sphere as your object of meditation, for example, gradually let your relaxed mind capture the orange marble. Imagine that orange marble is translucent, colorful, shiny and clean looking, captivating, relaxing and comforting for your mind to witness.

You may imagine that the orange marble is in front of you or that it has materialized in your own mind. This is up to the individual. In either case, concentrate on that orange marble, which is your object of meditation, without thinking, conceptualizing and judging. Merely concentrate and observe, witness the marble.

If you choose a small electric light as your object of meditation, for example, gradually let your relaxed mind capture the white light.

Imagine that this light is neither too bright nor too dim, and that it is illuminating and fixed, not fluctuating. It is captivating, relaxing and comforting for your mind to witness. Like the moon it has a cooling effect.

You may imagine that the bright white light is in front of you or that it has materialized in your own mind. This is up to the individual. In either case concentrate on that light, which is your object of meditation, without thinking, conceptualizing or judging. Merely concentrate and observe, witness the light.

A full image of Shakyamuni Buddha can be an actual object of meditation. The lotus flower as cushion symbolizes the purity of ethics. The Buddha's two legs are in the full lotus position and symbolize his unwavering determination not to release this position until he attains full Enlightenment.

His right hand is extended downward touching the earth, showing that he takes the earth as his witness for his attainment of full Enlightenment since no ordinary person can judge him. His left hand holds a dark bluish colored bowl almost overflowing with white nectar. That symbolizes fulfilling the aspirations of all beings to be happy.

His eyes are undistractedly gazing deep into the nature of reality. His ears are unusually long. His lips are very red and about to smile.

Then at his forehead is the *urna*, which is a single right turning hair that is extremely elastic, soft and highly fragrant, symbolizing his internal wisdom. The hair on his head is thick and black as a bumblebee. On the top of his head is the crown protrusion, two inches high, the physical sign of a fully enlightened being.

His skin color is like pure refined gold. His body is free of blemishes and any signs of aging. His body exhibits internal calmness, peacefulness, tranquility and serenity and his presence is very commanding, motivating, promising, inspiring, humbling and captivating.

Around his head is an aura. He is wearing a simple robe made from many pieces of cloth patched together, symbolizing renunciation and voluntary poverty for the sake of goodness.

CREATING CONDITIONS, CHOOSING OBJECTS

In case you cannot conjure or replicate the full physical image of the seated Buddha, you can build the image part by part as if you are an artist building a statue from clay. How might you build the image? You can divide the image in half, as shown below.

Then, using the lower one first, build from the lotus up to the chest. Then while holding that image, complete the object of meditation by building from chest up to the aura.

"Effortlessly "holding" the object of meditation in the field of your non conceptual awareness is meditation."

4

How to Meditate

IN GENERAL, SIT STILL, stop thinking, and start meditation by bringing the object of meditation to the forefront of your mind's eye and sustain concentration of mind exclusively on your selected object. In order to sustain concentration for a period of time—for more than an instant or a few seconds—the meditator requires the power of mindfulness and the power of vigilance.

In the above image, the candle flame is the selected object of meditation. The long arrow represents the mind meditating on the candle flame. There are two short arrows at the root of the mind meditating. One is mindfulness and the other is vigilance.

Sit in a comfortable posture in a relaxed state. Do not rush into the meditation like you jump into your bed. Recite some calming mantras or invoking prayers and let your mind be saturated by the feeling of compassion and any other feeling of spiritual inspiration.

It is also very helpful if you make a strong determination by saying in your mind, "I will never let my mind wander away from my original designated object of meditation." And then let yourself enter into the meditation by carrying the very force of the determination somewhere in the corner of your mind. This makes a real difference in your meditation.

If you are Buddhist and have taken Refuge, before sitting you are required to make three prostrations while reciting the prostration mantra or refuge formula each time you make a prostration. You should bring your ego, pride and sense of you being someone special down to zero level through the process of prostration, and reflect upon the meaning of prostration.

Upon sitting, if you are Buddhist, here you should repeat the short Refuge prayer, taking Refuge in the Buddha, Dharma, and Sangha as well as generate Bodhicitta from the depth of your heart. Bodhicitta is that state of mind rooted in the irreversible decision to attain Enlightenment for the sake of all sentient beings. Then let your mind be moistened with Refuge and Bodhicitta, carrying the force of this mind for the rest of your meditation practice.

Then take a moment to relax your mind by bringing your attention to your nostrils and be aware of your breath. Stay with the awareness of your breath for a few minutes.

Then gently let your object of meditation—for example, an image of Buddha, or a rose—appear in the field of your awareness. And then hold it in a relaxed way without projecting any of your emotions on it. The word "hold" means let it be there (in your awareness) without either conceptually adding something to it or conceptually subtracting from it. Let yourself be fully present in the intense awareness of the object of meditation. This mode of effortlessly "holding" the object of meditation in the field of your non conceptual awareness is meditation. When you are in that moment of holding, then you are meditating.

The mode of holding the object of meditation or awareness must have a balanced quality of mental stability and clarity. Mental stability refers to the one pointed focus of the mind. Mental clarity refers to the alertness or freshness of the mind, as well as the vivid appearance of the object of awareness to the meditating mind.

If you have meditated correctly over a long period of time, then surely you will experience that the objects of desire lose their driving force, freeing you from wanting and not wanting, liking and disliking them. This means those objects' imagined capability of making you happy when you get them or are with them is no longer important for you to be happy.

The objects of desire no longer have the power to cause you to be unhappy and upset when you don't get them, or when you are not with them, or when you no longer have them. Also your not getting them or not having them does not cause you to lose your sense of appreciation of having had them in the past. Your relationship with them is still intact, but the objects' driving force that makes you want/not want, like/dislike them is no longer there anymore. This is not a sign that something new has occurred within the object, but it is a clear sign that some changes have occurred in your own mind or perception.

When this change does not occur in you after years of meditation practice, it is a sign that something is wrong in your meditation and it is time for you to check it by consulting an experienced meditation master while leaving your ego behind.

Since meditation is cultivated only at the mental level and not at the sensory level, there should not be any sensory information that you are receiving through your five senses. The five senses are active but not engaged with their objects such as form, sound, smell, taste and touch.

"Active" means not dormant but not necessarily registering anything so as to cause thought. If the sense of hearing is indulging in sound, the mind might be stimulated and become engaged with the sound. This would prompt thought. In deep meditation, the connection between the mental consciousness and sensual world that is constituted of the objects of the five senses is temporarily disconnected or disengaged.

Every single meditation must have the two distinct qualities of stability and clarity. "Stability" here means the unwavering quality of the mind that is purposefully directed to a designated entity. "Clarity" here means an alertness or freshness of the mind being present in each moment within the continuum of the one pointed focus. The meditator is aware of the designated object without bringing emotional feeling to it.

Shamatha is a single pointed focus of mind with a very balanced quality of both stability and clarity conjoined with suppleness that prevents the meditator from getting physically and mentally exhausted and fatigued from sitting in meditation for long periods of time. Before you reach this stage of meditation—before you perfect Shamatha—you are often forced to stop your meditation due to experiences of physical and mental exhaustion or fatigue. When you reach this very balanced stage of meditation, then choose to discontinue your meditation whenever you like rather than ending it due to your physical and mental exhaustion.

Suppleness or *shin-jang* in Tibetan means "extremely refined in blissful nature." Suppleness is a blissful feeling arising from the most controlled and refined state of mind that is unstained and untouched by the ordinary mind's excitement, fantasies, hopes, fears and need to search for satisfaction from external sensual objects. Originally, suppleness is generated purely at the mental level and then it gradually permeates the entire physical body, creating a sense of lightness or agility, giving rise to a feeling that one can quite literally fly or jump distances that the ordinary human being cannot.

There are two types of suppleness: mental suppleness and physical suppleness. The two types of suppleness act as an antidote to the mental and physical dysfunctions that are obstacles to spiritual practice, particularly the practice of meditation.

Mental suppleness arises within the highly trained single pointed state of mind. It is then followed by physical suppleness. Mental suppleness is a spontaneous feeling of mental joy or bliss. This feeling of mental joy causes neither excitement nor attachment. It doesn't cause the meditator to have an obsession with that feeling of joy, of wanting more. Physical suppleness is an unusual feeling of agility or lightness within your body, which is due to the refined subtle wind movement throughout your body.

The common signs of physical suppleness are a sensation comparable to the gentle pressure you would feel if someone were to place a warm hand on your newly shaven head. Or a pleasurable sensation within the crown of your head where there was a little movement when you were a baby. As this sensation moves through the body, it creates a pleasant sensation of fullness throughout.

At the beginning, the mental suppleness and physical suppleness create a mounting pressure of mental joy as well as a physical sensation that makes you feel elated. Gradually this mounting pressure will settle down and the feeling of elatedness disappears. You have fully attained Shamatha from this point.

A single pointed focus of mind with a balanced quality of stability and clarity conjoined with suppleness is initially developed through the lengthy process of training your mind in what is called "the nine stages of mental abiding." Training in each stage takes long periods of time. At each stage your mental stability and clarity increase and become stronger and less subject to being destroyed by opposite states of mind such as distraction, excitement, wandering, wavering, dullness, laxity, sleepiness and lethargy.

Distraction is an aggressive thought, forcing the mind aimlessly to chase after the sensory object. This aggressive thought itself is induced and under the manipulation of either attachment or a repulsive feeling of dislike.

Excitement is a feeling of joy, looking forward to a desirable event or effect. This feeling of joy is under the influence of desirous attachment. Excitement can be a memory of past experience with a wish to relive that experience.

Wandering and wavering are the habits left behind by the force of distraction and excitement. These habits cause the mind to find false comfort in roaming here and there like a mad dog roaming the streets.

There are two types of distraction and excitement. They are gross and subtle. Gross mental distraction and excitement kidnap your mental focus or attention away from your designated object of meditation and attach to something else, preventing you from doing what you are supposed to be doing during that sitting moment.

Subtle mental distraction and excitement slowly lead to ideation, which compromises the intensity of the mind's mode of holding the object of meditation. In other words, the lack of intensity within the stability leaves room for the mind to be divided in its awareness of the object, although the mind never turns away from its designated object.

Dullness and laxity are the inwardly withdrawn qualities of a mind that lacks alertness, freshness and clarity. The lack of freshness of the mind is caused by a feeling of heaviness or cloudiness over your head. This feeling of heaviness can be caused by a lack of sleep, eating excessive or heavy, oily food, eating garlic or onions, being in an environment with a hot temperature, sitting in a dark room, being physically exhausted from overwork, being mentally fatigued from over thinking, and other causes. In Hinduism, garlic and onion are the external cause for the arising of internal cognitive heaviness and sloth, which is called *tamas*.

The feeling of lethargy or heaviness over your head induces a cognitive darkness, destroying the freshness or the alertness of your mind towards its apprehended object. The intensity of your mind's ability to hold the object of meditation is lost or slackened.

The Nine Stages of Calm Abiding

Now we will examine closely the nine stages for gradual development of mental abiding or shamatha. During the first three of the nine stages of training in meditation, your mental focus is too weak and poor. So, you should simply emphasize building good, strong mental stability during your training in the first three stages. And do not be overly concerned with mental clarity.

At the fourth stage, your mental focus or stability is pretty good and strong. But still your mental clarity is too weak and poor.

During the fourth, fifth and sixth stages, you should emphasize the building of good mental clarity. By the end of the fourth stage you have overcome gross distraction. By the end of the fifth stage you have overcome gross laxity. By the end of the sixth stage you have overcome subtle distraction or excitement.

But up to the end of the sixth stage, your mental stability and clarity have not reached a balanced state. So, at the seventh stage, you should simply work on balancing the mental stability and clarity. By the end of the seventh stage you have balanced mental stability and clarity and have overcome subtle laxity.

Then you enter the eighth stage, which is called "single pointed with effort." On the eighth stage your meditation is not yet a free ride, which means you need some degree of conscious effort in starting the meditation and in maintaining the single pointed state of mind by being vigilant.

When you reach the ninth stage, your meditation is now a free ride requiring no effort, but still it is not complete Shamatha until it conjoins with suppleness or *shin-jang*.

In order to attain true Shamatha, you must train your mind in a systematic way with a degree of learned or trained control over it. Otherwise, although you might initially experience very good meditative awareness of the visualized object by accident, as long as your mind is not properly trained and controlled your meditative awareness is not very useful or reliable.

Until you reach the ninth mental stage, it is extremely important to follow the proper sequential order of the mental stages, just as you must lay proper foundations for a house if you are going to construct strong and reliable walls.

The nine stages of mental abiding are:

1. Fixing the mind
2. Fixation with some continuity
3. Re-fixation
4. Close fixation
5. Subduing
6. Pacifying
7. Fully pacifying
8. Single pointed with effort
9. Meditative equipoise or effortless single pointedness

Fixing the Mind

In this stage, you are working simply on fixing your mind on the object of meditation. An object of meditation is a mental picture (for example an image of Buddha or a rose), which your mind is going to rest or focus upon without conceptualizing. Here at this first stage, finding the object of awareness and fixing your mind on the object of meditation are too difficult. Bringing the mind onto the object of meditation is too difficult because when the mind is about to fix, thought interferes and the mind gets carried away by that force, or the attempt to make the mind capture the object of meditation is too difficult. For example, balancing an egg on top of another egg seems impossible. There is no time when that egg sits on the other egg. The balance seems impossible to achieve.

The moment you have managed to fix your mind on the object of meditation you lose it. After training over a long period of time your effort of fixing your mind on the object becomes much easier and quicker. When this happens you have reached the end of the first stage, which is called fixing the mind. However, keeping the fixation of your mind on the object of meditation is too short. The effort of fixing the mind on the object of meditation is now really easy, but keeping the fixation with continuity is too difficult and too disappointing.

At this stage, you will notice that your mind is congested with too many thoughts, more than when you were not meditating. You might also notice that the thoughts are unusually aggressive, demanding, and pushing for you to chase after them.

Actually the thoughts are not increasing any more than when you are not meditating. Really, you are becoming more aware of their arising, especially thoughts unrelated and unnecessary to what you are actually doing at that very moment. This is an indication that you are dealing with your mind in order to direct its focus to a designated and observed object, the object of meditation.

When you are not meditating you might find your mind very supple and pliant. But when you actually try and apply it to an object of meditation you are able to see how wild and unruly it becomes. The restless monkey-like and mad elephant-like wild and unruly mind is extremely difficult to tame, discipline, and correct. The more effort you exert to tame it, the wilder your mind seems to become. Your mind can barely catch a glimpse of your object of meditation owing to the intensity of your inner chattering and habits of aimless mental wanderings.

Fixation with Some Continuity

After training persistently, when your effort of maintaining the fixation of your mind on the object of meditation becomes stronger and longer with some continuity, let's say 3-4 minutes, then you have reached the second stage, which is called fixation with some continuity. But here you often fail to bring your mind back to the object of meditation quickly due to being unaware that you have lost it. You have already spent a long time with your mind wandering before you actually become aware of losing the object of meditation, and you have to painfully struggle to bring it back to the object.

Re-Fixing the Mind

After training persistently, when you get to the point where your effort to bring your mind back to the object of meditation becomes easy, and you are capable of being immediately aware of losing the object of meditation, then you have reached the third stage, which is called re-fixing the mind.

Close Fixation

After training persistently, when you get to the point where you are not subject to losing the object of meditation though the clarity of the fixated mind is still very weak, then you have reached the fourth stage, which is called close fixation. From here you must emphasize more the building of clarity by means of getting rid of the lethargic feeling in your mind. The maturity of your mindfulness has reached its peak, and you will never lose the object of meditation, because you have overcome the gross mental distraction and excitement.

As stated previously, gross distraction is an aggressive thought stemming from an attachment or aversion that kidnaps your attention away from where your mental attention was originally directed. It forces your mind to roam like a mad dog without any purposeful destination to be reached. Since excitement is a feeling of joy of looking forward to an anticipated event, it has an element within it that causes the person's mind to be agitated or restless. You are prone to gross distraction and excitement if you have dominant problems of attachment to sensual objects and sensual pleasure. So, it is important to reduce the intensity of your attachment to sensual objects and sensual pleasure.

Attachment is an emotional feeling of intimacy with another person or object with the sole hope of them making you happy. This hope of them making you happy is based on your mistaken perception of seeing them with an inherent quality and therefore capable of making you happy as long as you are with them or as long as you have them in your possession.

This feeling of attachment not only makes you very unhappy when you don't have them in your possession, it makes you unhappy with them even when you have them in your possession. Why? Because your attachment to them demands from them a kind of happiness that is more than what they are capable of providing you. You are never satisfied with what they can provide. You will never be happy or satisfied with them because your attachment keeps telling you that what you get from them is not what the I (attachment) is looking for from them. And then you keep forcing on the other person or object the hope that they will increase your pleasure and satisfaction.

Actually the way you are forcing on them is nothing other than squeezing out the object's capability of making you happy and giving you zero pleasure, leaving you wanting more of pleasure and satisfaction that is stronger and greater.

What is the difference between attachment and compassion? Like attachment, compassion is also an emotional intimacy with other people and beings, but compassion has the sole purpose and hope of you making them happy, rather than them making you happy. At the very emotional intimate level, there is a similarity between attachment and compassion, but they are totally different when it comes to their functional level.

Attachment's function is to make you very unhappy when you don't get what you are expecting from the other person or object for your personal gain and interest. Attachment also makes you unhappy even when you get the things you are expecting, because of not getting them in the precise way you want.

In contrast, compassion's function is making you happy and joyful about what you are doing to make others happy and how others are profitably gaining from your help. Your feeling of compassion will never make you unhappy due to your not getting something from others for your personal gain and interest.

You must not mistake compassion for attachment. Their difference is very clear from their functional aspect.

Subduing

After training persistently, when you get to the point where your mind gains the maximum intensity of mental stability, but the intensity of mental clarity is not yet that intense, then you have reached the fifth stage, which is called subduing. Still the power of vigilance is not fully mature, and therefore there is a risk of your meditation being stained by subtle laxity as well as subtle distraction.

Vigilance is a quality of the meditating mind, not a separate entity. Vigilance, retrospection, and introspection are all used interchangeably, and are like the mind watching the mind, the power of self awareness. The power of vigilance is the power of being instantly aware that you have lost the object of meditation or are about to lose it and bringing the mind back to the object or preventing losing it.

From here you have to overcome subtle distraction. Subtle distraction means that though your awareness is still very much on the object of meditation, some portion of your mind is making or has already made contact with something else other than the chosen object of awareness. It is almost as if the mind is holding two different objects at the same time and your awareness is not 100% on the designated object. At the end of the fifth stage, subduing, this problem of divided awareness is now gone.

Pacifying

After training persistently, you will get to the point where your mind gains more clarity by getting rid of lethargic feelings that cloud your mind. When the strength of your mind, which is holding the object of meditation, becomes a little intense then you have reached the sixth stage, which is called pacifying.

Now you have overcome the gross laxity. Gross laxity is a mind in its sinking state or a state that is too relaxed, causing you to lose the mind's clarity or freshness. Laxity is the gloominess or cloudiness of the subjective mind that holds the object of meditation.

In other words, laxity is a lack of fresh subjective clarity. Subjective clarity is the fresh vibrancy of the meditating mind. In this case "vibrancy" is the freshness, alertness and lucidity of the aliveness of the mind. Here "gloominess" is meant in the cognitive sense rather than the emotional sense.

Fully Pacifying

After training persistently, when you get to the point where your mind gains a full intensity of mental clarity by getting rid of the risk of staining your meditation by subtle laxity, then you have reached the seventh stage, which is called fully pacifying. At this point the power of the vigilance has fully matured.

Now you have overcome subtle laxity. Subtle laxity involves a lack of intensity in the subjective clarity. Subtle laxity is extremely difficult to recognize and is very difficult to overcome.

Single Pointed

After training persistently, when you get to the point where your mind becomes single pointed with a balanced quality of intense stability and intense clarity but still needs some degree of effort in starting and maintaining the meditation (it has not yet become a free ride), then you have entered the eighth stage, which is called single pointed with effort.

Meditative Equipoise

After training persistently, when you get to the point where the single pointed mind with a perfect balanced quality of intense stability and intense clarity becomes a free ride—without there being any need of effort, no matter how long you are going to remain in the meditative state—then you have entered the ninth stage, which is called meditative equipoise or effortless single pointedness.

The effortless single pointedness becomes complete Shamatha when it conjoins with suppleness and serves as a perfect basis for the development of the penetrative insight of Vipassana.

At the beginning the suppleness creates some degree of elatedness in the meditating mind, and then it gradually settles down, causing the mind to be just so supple. This feeling of elation has a slight element of excitement or an element of causing the mind to have a tendency to become excited, and that brings emotional damage within the very strength of stability. The true suppleness will not arise until the feeling of elation completely settles down to zero. In other words, the feeling of elation goes away.

Hindrances to Meditation

You cannot perfect Shamatha meditation without fully overcoming the gross and subtle distraction and the gross and subtle laxity. You must know how to apply a remedy to them once they arise during your meditation. You must work on not letting them reside in you when you are meditating with pretty good stability and clarity within the relaxed state of awareness of the designated object.

In the beginning, an act of applying a remedy to the distraction and laxity itself throws you out of your meditation. Which means you are no longer in a meditative state. So in the beginning, choose to sit in several shorter meditation sessions a day, and work on better quality of meditation. This is the best and most wise decision.

The practice of Shamatha is much more than merely resting your mind in a relaxed state free from annoyance or distraction by external provoking circumstances (or your inner attracted or repulsed response to them). The proper cultivation of Shamatha meditation is a mode of your mind's resting in an awareness state with a useful quality of nonthinking stability/stillness, as well as mindfulness and the alertness of being vigilant.

The quality of stability and clarity that determines the calm resting mind as Shamatha will not occur unless you tirelessly work on recognizing and eliminating the gross and subtle distractions, excitements, laxity and dullness. These are the major obstacles for the development of mental stability and mental clarity. You must work on eliminating them by applying the right antidote while you are sitting in meditation. The antidote is detecting the presence of the hindrances of the meditation and immediately correcting them instead of letting those hindrances simply continue to be there. For example, if the hindrance is sleepiness and sleepiness is dominating your mind, the meditator needs to detect the sleepiness, immediately detect it as a hindrance, and correct it by means of refreshing and uplifting the mind without discontinuing the meditation. It is also possible to discontinue your meditation from time to time in order to adopt an antidotal application to subdue the distractions and laxity.

How to Find the Object of Meditation

As I mentioned above, you have the liberty to choose the object of your meditation. You should choose the object of meditation according to your mental inclination and needs. Any object that naturally gives you a sense of emotional contentment and comfort is the best.

Here I would like to suggest to you a specific object for your meditation. The reason is that, in general, your mind has a chronic habit of chasing after sensory experiences and their objects as well as following the aspect of the object (characteristics of the object such as pleasing sound). As long as your mind is chasing after the sensory experiences and the aspect of the external object, you don't have any control over your mind and thoughts.

One of the purposes of meditation is to gain control over your mind, thoughts, and emotions, so that the mind will not chase or follow the sensory experiences and the aspects of external objects. Your mind and the emotions chase after the objects' aspects that seem capable of affecting your personal life. When you are meditating, you are not letting your mind behave in this way—that is chasing after sensory objects, thoughts, emotions. You are controlling your mind by restraining it from chasing after the aspects of different objects.. You are disciplining your mind, causing it to remain focused on its original object as it was in the beginning.

Therefore, there is special meaning in using a specific object with distinct features. My suggestion on a specific object of meditation is the image of the Buddha with four distinct features:

1. Fixed shape—of normal human form
2. Fixed size—four inches high or as small as your thumb
3. Fixed color—refined and golden, free from any spots or dots
4. Fixed location—seated on a lotus cushion

Use this specific image of the Buddha as an object of your meditation. This object you can call the original, designated, selected, and purposeful object of meditation. When you choose this type of specific object you have made a commitment in your mind to be just with it and not to chase after and engage with something else other than the thing that is being designated.

When you use the image of the Buddha with these four distinct features as the object of your meditation, you must have a sense of contentment and emotional comfort with it. If you are discontent with it then you will end up separating from it. Divorcing from the object of your meditation once it has been designated is a serious mistake for the successful practice of meditation. So, it is also important to cultivate a sense of contentment with the image of the Buddha in terms of being comfortable with the Buddha through your sense of devotional intimate connection with him. Reflect on the physical qualities of the Buddha. For example, his serene sitting position is very captivating and very inspiring.

During the actual cultivation of Shamatha meditation, your original object of meditation will frequently change its aspect and features. Your mind will habitually chase or follow those changes. The aspect of the object changes in terms of its shape, size, color, and location. As long as those changes are occurring and as long as you let your mind chase after them without making any effort to correct the object by making it return back to its original state, you are not meditating at all.

You must be aware of the changes of the object and must make an effort to stop your mind from chasing them. You must make the object return back to its original state and rest your awareness on it once again. Do not be concerned about the length of time of resting your awareness on it. Rather, you should be more concerned about the stability of the object of meditation. Here stability means fixed or objective unchanging entity. Actually the object of meditation itself is not changing. It is your mind that causes the object to change its aspect in four ways—shape, size, color, and location.

These four ways of changing the aspect of the object are what I call "the four errors" of your mind. But normally you blame the object for those changes. An object does not harbor the intention to change its physical aspect. Rather it is your mind causing the object to change.

Always keeping the root object or the original object of meditation is extremely important for the cultivation of Shamatha. Your mind must not chase or follow the object's changes caused by your mind and must return to rest on the original object.

In addition to the object with those four features—fixed shape, fixed size, fixed color, and fixed location—it is also very useful to imagine the object with a nature of light or being bright and radiant, as well as extremely dense or heavy. The density of the object helps you to stabilize the mind, because it helps your mind to feel like it is being pressed or pressured by the density of the object, and this holds the mind's attention.

In other words, the density of the object creates a sense of heaviness or weight over your mind, making your mind less inclined to sneak out here and there. The density of the object also gives the feeling of pulling your mind into the object of meditation in which your mind is stabilizing with a degree of concentration. The brightness of the object helps the freshness of your mind because it helps you to eliminate the darkness or cognitive gloominess of your mind.

You cultivate Shamatha by focusing your mind single pointedly on the object of meditation—for example, an image of the Buddha with four distinct features as explained above. After some time the object of meditation (mental picture of the Buddha) becomes real to you. You start having a sense of an interaction between you and the mental picture of the Buddha.

This sense of interaction will be a bit like some kind of conversation between you and the mental picture of the Buddha is actually happening or about to happen soon. If you are using a rose as an object of meditation, then your sense of interaction will be a bit like you being able to smell the flower. Or the smell of the rose is pervading your surroundings, and you are almost ready to say "wow" because the aroma is so sweet.

You should not be excited about these experiences. You should simply continue your meditation without the feelings of curiosity and anticipation. The continuation of the meditation will help you to arrive at the point where you no longer feel yourself as separate from the object of meditation. Your previous feeling of you and your mind over here as an observer and the object of meditation as an observed object over there will have disappeared.

You and the object of meditation become one. "One" does not mean one at the physical level, as this is impossible anyway. What it means is one at the mental level. This is because your experience of you as an observer and the object of meditation as an observed object have now merged. The feeling of the observer as something over here—on this side—and the observed object as something over there—on the other side—has vanished. In other words, the duality of the subjective mind and the objective focal object has vanished.

What is really left in you is the mere non dual awareness of the image of the Buddha. All of the other minds—thoughts, feeling, emotions, recognition, sensations including the sense consciousness—are either in their latent state or in a totally disengaged state in relation to their usual objects.

Your sense of who you are, what you are, is no longer there. You are not a beneficiary of nor a loser of anything. All of your life's puzzles have vanished and you become completely free from every single trace of who you are, what you are, and what you have gone through up until now. You are being fully present in the intense awareness of the object of meditation. Your awareness, experience, and your sense of being are not divided into the past, present, and the future.

You have fully attained Shamatha when this non dual awareness is conjoined with the mental and physical suppleness. Your mind becomes supple, pliant, and serviceable and is now free from mental and physical dysfunction. Mental and physical dysfunctions are not, in this case, illnesses or sicknesses of the mind or body. They are only the non serviceability of the mind and body. If you employ the mind and the body too hard, then you will feel some kind of lethargic or exhausted feeling as well as have the tendency of getting sick.

The mental and physical dysfunctions limit your capability to reach or accomplish something. The mental and physical dysfunctions are like something that is installed or injected in your mind and body by the force of your karma and delusion and are there from the moment of conception.

Lus sem kyi gnas ngan len, in Tibetan, means mental and physical dysfunction. They are naturally conducive to the arising of the non virtuous activities of life. In other words, they are conducive to unwholesome performances of the body, speech, and mind, and non conducive to wholesome performances of the body, speech, and mind. That includes the practice of meditation.

When you have trained the nine stages and attained Shamatha, the mind of Shamatha then perfectly serves as a basis for the development of penetrative insight meditation or Vipassana.

More on How to Find the Object of Meditation

As stated earlier, the object of meditation does not mean a physical object sitting in front of you so that you can look at it directly with your eyes. An object of meditation is a mere mental picture—in the example we have been using, the mental picture of the Buddha. It is a duplicate image or picture of the real object that you can see, touch, and smell. It is like a photocopy taken or printed by your mind, and it stays in your mind or within the field of your awareness.

Finding an object of meditation is a process of generating the image of the real object, such as the Buddha, in your mind without using your senses. In other words, it is a process of building or constructing the duplicate image of the real object in your own mind with the object's detailed characteristics. Once you have built the image of the real object, then you should make it stay in your mind like a reflection of the real object stays in a mirror. The duplicate image of the object is something like a reflection of the object. Your mind is something like the mirror.

You must have a clear idea or understanding about the real object, such as what the object looks like as well as its unique features, prior to generating the image of the real object in your mind.

Let's use, for instance, the Buddha. Note what the Buddha looks like and the sitting position, throne or lotus cushion, hand gestures or mudras, begging bowl, robe, skin color, undistracted gaze of his fresh eyes, urna (an extremely fine coiled piece of hair between the eyebrows, which signifies the inner wisdom eye of reality), crown protrusion (which signifies the full attainment of Enlightenment), and aura (a rainbow colored circle of light around his head). The Buddha who is in the nature of compassion, wisdom, love, and care, is right there just for you and your needs.

Based on this understanding of the Buddha, you should hold the image of the Buddha with those distinct features and physical characteristics in your mind or in the field of your awareness. The way to build the image of the Buddha is like a craftsman builds the statue of Buddha from a well prepared piece of clay. You should build it part by part and stage by stage like an artist builds the statue part by part and stage by stage.

When you have completed the construction of the Buddha image in your mind, then mentally try to feel it, such as where the hands are resting, how the legs are in a lotus position, where the urna is, and where he is seated until you get a clear sense of the image of the Buddha. In a similar way a blind person gets a sense of what the object looks like (except for the color) in his mind by touching it with his hands.

Once you get the clear image of the Buddha in your mind, then simply "hold" it in your awareness without conceptualizing and without making any effort to make it clearer. "Simply hold" means let it just be there in the field of your awareness. Let yourself be fully present in the intense awareness of the image of the Buddha. Try to remain in that state for a period of time, say ten to fifteen minutes. Train yourself until the act or the mode of remaining in that state becomes natural to you and brings you a sense of comfort.

If you are using the natural beauty of a rose as your object of meditation, then you should proceed as stated above. You should go through the process of building a specific type of rose, for example a newly blossomed white rose with 18 petals— with eight petals on the outer circle, six petals in the middle circle, four petals in the inner circle, and a pink center. Such a rose might be sitting in a crystal flower vase on your small practice table. When you have completed the construction of the flower to the point where you can see it in its entirety, then you simply "hold" it in your awareness without conceptualizing and without making any effort to make it more clear, etc.

Again, to simply "hold" means to let it just be there in the field of your awareness. In other words, let yourself be fully present in the intense awareness of the image of the rose.

Try to remain in that state for a period of time, say ten to fifteen minutes. Make sure always to retain or restore the original state of the rose without there being the occurrence of any physical changes such as its color, shape, size, and location.

You should train in the cultivation of the single pointed non conceptual awareness of the rose until the mode of your remaining in that state becomes natural to you, bringing with it a sense of comfort. At this point you may have a sense of smell of the rose. Your mental picture of the flower will begin to serve the same functions of an actual flower.

If you are using the breath as an object of meditation, then you should follow these instructions: Gently bring your mental focus to your nostrils. Try to feel the tactile physical sensation at your nostril area when the air is coming in and going out. Stay with it for a few minutes. Then shift your focus from the tactile physical sensation to the breath, and be aware of the breath. To make your awareness of the breath strong, you should count your breaths while sustaining the awareness of the breath.

Count the breath up to the number ten. When you reach ten, then do the reverse count from ten to one. Count exhalation and inhalation as one, exhalation and inhalation as two, exhalation and inhalation as three, etc.

Do not conceptualize when you are counting your breath such as "Now I am exhaling and now I am inhaling. This is outgoing air and this is incoming air. Exhaling air is longer than the incoming air and incoming air is shorter than the outgoing air."

Also, you should not make any effort to control your breath. Let your breath be normal in its natural rhythm.

When you reach counting from ten to one, then stop counting and merely rest in the intense awareness of the breath for five minutes. After five minutes you should try to shift your awareness from your breath to the "interval gap" between the incoming air and the outgoing air. There is a natural time gap between the exhalation and inhalation. You should try to use the gap that naturally exists between the incoming and outgoing air as the final resting place of your awareness. Rest your awareness in the gap for a period of ten minutes.

This interval is merely a short time or a space gap and there is nothing to be confirmed nor to be negated. However when you are resting in that gap, you are still slightly aware of the incoming and outgoing air somewhere in the corner of your awareness of the gap. Your whole effort and emphasis of the awareness should be on the gap between the incoming and outgoing air.

Whenever you meditate, it is extremely important to sustain your mind's alertness, mindfulness, vigilance, and relaxed concentrated state, which is focused on the object of observation or meditation. In this case, the breath is the object of observation (at the beginning), and the interval or gap is a final object of observation.

If you're using your own mind as an object of meditation, then you should follow these instructions: Relax your mind by not bringing anything into the field of your awareness. Let go of all your thoughts, emotions, ideas, concepts, and the eight worldly concerns of gain and loss, happiness and sorrow, praise and blame, fame and infamy.

In the beginning of your meditation, you will find too many thoughts and emotions are arising, one right after another. You will see that your mind is none other than the constant flow of thoughts and emotions. Thoughts are arising one after another, and the first thought dissolves into the second thought. There is no time gap between the first thought and the second thought.

After some time, you will get to the point where the thoughts settle down pretty well and they are not arising one after another as they did earlier. At this point you will notice a "time gap" between the first thought and the second thought—a time gap in the sense that the first thought had ceased and the second or later thought had not yet arisen. In between those thoughts, there is a brief moment of pure awareness that has a quality of clarity and luminosity. This brief moment of pure awareness is non selective, non discriminatory, and unbiased. It is a state of mere knowingness with the quality of transparency. This transparency of the awareness is the essential nature of your mind.

It is a bit like when you stop the muddy running water from where it is going to and where it is coming from. The muddy water between the two places (where it is going to and where it is coming from) naturally becomes still, clear, and transparent as impurities settle out. The water can now be allowed to reveal its nature of transparency.

Once you reach this point, then you should simply rest your mind in that pure awareness without making any attempt to see what is there and what it is.

The effort that is required prevents any thoughts from arising that corrupt the quality of the mere knowing entity of awareness.

When you become more familiar with the mind as a mere knowing entity that is free of accepting and rejecting (which are the habits of a conceptual mind), then you are already fully introduced to the essential nature of your mind—mere knowing, clarity, and luminosity—and all you have to do is sustain the unbroken, unobstructed, and unaltered continuity of the state of the mind as a mere knowing entity.

“ When your mind and body are not cooperating because of sleepiness and physical tiredness, stop the meditation and do these other practices. ”

5

Other Supportive Practices

Merit and Purification

THERE ARE CERTAIN PRACTICES that definitely contribute to your meditation practice. The practices of the accumulation of merit and the purification of negativity and karmic obstructions are extremely important for the successful meditation practice.

Merit is not credit, nor is it an appreciative expression or a gesture from another person towards your good deeds. Merit is positive energy. It takes place in your own mind by your own positive actions of body, speech, and mind. It acts as a fertilizer for the proper growth of your spiritual practice. It nurtures and incubates your spiritual seeds and Dharma understanding. It is a serious mistake if you don't pay attention or engage in the practices of the accumulation of merit and the purification of negativity and karmic obstructions, because these are essential for your successful meditation practice.

There are many practices that you can engage in for the accumulation of merit. The most effective practices that accumulate huge amounts of merit are the practice of Guru Yoga, and the Thirty-Seven Point or the Seven Point Mandala Offering with proper visualization of the Merit Field along with the understanding of the Buddhist cosmic structure of the entire world system. There are also other virtuous activities like making full body prostrations while reciting the prostration mantra. Also rejoicing and taking delight in others' merits, virtuous deeds, and spiritual accomplishments without the slightest feeling of jealousy and competitiveness will accumulate huge amounts of merit within one single moment of rejoicing. Lama Tsong-Khapa once said that one who accumulates a huge amount of merit with very little effort is one who rejoices in others' meritorious and virtuous deeds. This is highly recommended.

There are many practices that purify your negativity and karmic obscurations. The three most effective practices for the purification of negativity and karmic obscurations are the recitation of the *tung-shak* (purification of ethical and moral downfalls), the names of the purification Buddhas, and the recitation of the hundred seed syllable mantra of Vajrasattva.

These practices are very effective for the accumulation of merit as well as for the purification of negativity and karmic obscurations that you have created over many lifetimes. These practices have also been tested and highly recommended by the great masters of past generations.

Most of these practices, both in Tibetan and English, can be found in my practice manual book called *A Sharp Weapon for the Total Elimination of Inner Darkness Caused by the Delusions and Distorted Emotions* and in the *Nyer Kho Ngo Mo Chey Tu Shug So*. The *Nyer Kho Ngo Mon Chey Tu Shug So* is a collection of essential prayers and mantras to be used in your daily Dharma practice to make it complete and effective.

Most of those practices can be done during your post meditation period. When you are sometimes too sleepy and cannot do meditation, then you should make prostrations or recite the hundred syllable mantra instead. Don't be so rigid in your meditation. When your mind and body are not cooperating because of feelings of sleepiness and physical tiredness, stop the meditation and do these other practices.

Physical Health

Your physical health is also very important to your Dharma practice. Proper physical exercise of hatha yoga is designed to build physical health to retain the psychic channels with their natural flow of vital energy and *prana* or psychic air.

Hatha Yoga and Prostrations

The practice of physical exercise of hatha yoga and prostrations, as well as certain types of visualization, are for cleansing the toxins that reside in your body, which are caused by the force of negative thoughts and emotions of extreme depression, sadness, a deep sense of loss, hatred, and other emotions that have natural destructive potential.

Both hatha yoga and prostrations must be practiced by bringing your mind into a virtuous state, or at least into a state of calm, free from negative thoughts and emotions. In other words, you unite the body and mind while maintaining some degree of spiritual awareness in a spiritual atmosphere.

You should not practice hatha yoga and prostrations merely for the benefit of your physical body with only a concern of having an attractive appearance in the eyes of others. Both hatha yoga and prostrations help to bring physical wellbeing, which has a positive effect on your inner spiritual training and meditation practice.

The purpose of life is happiness. Happiness can be divided into two parts: physical and mental happiness. For the Buddhist practitioner inner mental wellbeing is more important than physical wellbeing. Inner mental wellbeing cannot be gained from an external material source. It can be gained only through mental and spiritual training. Long lasting inner mental happiness can occur through the practice of meditation and wisdom realizing the ultimate truth of reality, which primarily refers to emptiness. The detailed explanation of emptiness can be found below in the Vipassana section.

When you have the inner mental wellbeing gained through meditation, then it is possible that your physical pain can be weakened or overwhelmed by the force of your mental wellbeing; whereas your mental and emotional pain cannot be numbed or weakened by the force of your physical wellbeing gained from an external material source. Therefore, your practice of hatha yoga and prostrations should be aimed not only at gaining some physical fitness, but even more as an aid to your emotional wellbeing and spiritual awareness of reality.

The practice of prostrations in everyday life is one of the crucial parts of the Buddhist training. In general, there are many benefits of making prostrations. However, the following are the most prominent:

- purification of negativities and karmic obstructions created over the series of past and present lifetimes;
- accumulation of merit for uninterrupted spiritual growth and to gain swift spiritual realization;
- planting the seeds of the three kayas within your mindstream;
- releasing physical and mental tension and knots;
- unblocking and clearing out the psychic nerve system and other channels through which the vital energy moves;
- creating lightness, agility, flexibility, or even suppleness by getting rid of physical lethargy;
- burning fats in your body and helping to increase your digestive function;
- curing many chronic illnesses primarily caused by karmic debts; and
- reshaping your body and mind, since prostration is good exercise in an ordinary physical sense, and in an ultimate sense it is a yogic training of body and mind, to lay down the groundwork for a sound base of spiritual growth.

The practice of hatha yoga, too, has many of these benefits if you do it with a proper spiritual awareness by bringing mind and body into perfect union in the present moment.

There are two types of prostrations: short and full body prostrations. When you do the short prostration, you touch five parts of your body on the ground—two knees, two palms, and forehead. When you do the full body prostration, you touch the whole body to the ground by stretching your hands straight out in front of you, and then using your hands to make the prostration gesture to your crown. If it is possible, you should make an effort to do the full body prostration.

From my own experience, I can say that the practice of prostrations along with the mindful recitation of the hundred syllable Vajrasattva purification mantra and the names of thirty-five purification Buddhas is extremely powerful for the advancement of spiritual training. I do my prostration practice between 4:00 a.m. and 6:15 a.m. every day. It makes a huge difference in my main Dharma practice, which I do between 7:00 a.m. and 9:15 a.m., after which I begin my daily activities such as reading, writing, cleaning, meeting and seeing people for their Dharma guidance. I highly recommend you do a certain number of prostrations every day apart from your main practice, whatever it may be.

The prostration mantra helps to multiply and increase the number and force of prostrations into thousands, though you actually make just one. Below is the prostration mantra to be recited when you do prostrations. Recite this mantra each time you do one prostration.

OM NAMO MANJUSHIRI YE! NAMO SUSHRIYE! NAMO UTAMMA SHRIYE SOHA!

Regarding Food

There are several types of food or nourishment mentioned in the Buddhist teaching of the Abhidharma. "Morsel food" is the regular or gross food that you consume that has particular color, shape, smell, taste and texture. A part of this food goes into your system carrying a nurturing force, and part of it becomes waste that needs to be discharged from your body. You should eat morsel food very moderately when you practice hatha yoga and prostrations. Overconsumption of this food makes your body and mind lethargic and causes a kind of cloud over your mind. It also hinders the natural flow of energy in your body, which eventually causes physical illness.

Among the several other types of food mentioned in the Abhidharma are 1) the food of sleep and 2) the food of meditation. The first, sleep, has a nourishing power in your body by allowing your body to be fully rested without the disturbances of a restless mind and its thoughts and emotions. If you ask why we need sleep, the answer is because your body needs rest from your restless mind and its aggressive demands for its unlimited needs. A baby needs more sleep than food for physical maturation and nourishment. The second, meditation, is the calm, peaceful, tranquil, focused, unwavering state of mind with a deep feeling of relaxation from your core of being that nourishes your body. Therefore, a true meditator does not need as much sleep as a non meditator does, because meditation gives maximum rest to your body like sleep gives rest.

Offerings

Many of you make external material offerings before the enlightened beings, but perhaps not correctly. External material offerings consist of such things as water, flowers, candles, incense, fruit, and musical sound.

It is extremely important that the material offering should not be obtained by wrong and deceptive means. Anything that is obtained from wrong and deceptive means cannot be a delightful offering to enlightened beings. The offering material must be obtained through right and wholesome means.

The correct way to make offerings before the enlightened beings is with mindful recitation of the following mantra called "mantra of essence of interdependent co-existence." This mantra helps to multiply and increase your material offerings made before the enlightened beings. You should recite this mantra with mindfulness while or after making the offerings, with a fresh understanding of conventional reality as a miraculous result of interdependent co-arising.

Other Supportive Practices

NAMO RATNA TRAYAYA! NAMO BHAGAVATE!
BENZAH SARA TRAMA DHANEY!
TATHAGATAYA! ARYA HATEY SAMYA SAMBUD-
DHA YA! TEYA THA! OM BENZEY BENZEY! MAHA
BENZEY! MAHA BHI YA BENZEY! MAHA TEZO
BENZEY! MAHA BHODHI MENDRO PAKSAM! TRAMA
NEY! SAWA KAMA! AVA RATNA! BHI SHO DANEY
BENZEY! SO HA!

Then recite this mantra three times: OM AH HUNG!

OM—purifies the impurities of color, odor and taste of the material offering substances such as fruits, flowers, cookies, and so forth

AH—transforms the offering substance into ambrosia and nectar of the wisdom of emptiness

HUNG—multiplies the offering substance boundlessly and reaches beyond the limitations of your dualistic mind

“ The state of Nirvana can only be developed by the unified practice of Shamatha and Vipassana meditation. ”

6

Ultimate Analysis: "Abiding in the Very Conclusion"

ONCE YOU HAVE ATTAINED true Shamatha meditation, you can easily develop some minor psychic powers such as the ability to recall your previous lives, read other people's minds, and see future events before their actual occurrence. These are not particularly valuable in themselves, but they surely provide you with a solid basis of confidence in the laws of karma and both stabilize and strengthen your practice. The development of psychic powers, such as clairvoyance and other powers, are not the real purpose of Shamatha meditation. The real purpose of Shamatha meditation is to serve as a basis for the proper development of penetrative insight into the true nature of reality. The true nature of reality refers to emptiness, or *shunyata* in Sanskrit.

Emptiness is the actual mode in which things and objects come into existence, with a total lack of inherent mode of existence from their own nature. "Mode of being" is not just interdependent arising. It is also the mere absence of objective reality. But that does not mean nothing exists. Things exist through the process of being dependent on designation. The process of being dependent on designation is the most subtle meaning of dependent arising, as I will explain below.

Shamatha meditation that is divorced from Vipassana or penetrative insight meditation into the nature of reality in itself will not bring any higher spiritual realization or awareness. Shamatha alone cannot defeat your inner enemy force of delusions, confusion and the fundamental ignorance of reality. The fundamental ignorance of reality refers to the misconception of self–I–mine as an entity having inherent existence, and the misperception of the world around you as other than you, as separate from you and as having inherent existence.

It is the misconception of self that divides the whole world into two: the world of "I" and "you," or the world of "self" and the world of "other." From this false notion of self and other arise the afflictive emotions of attachment to the world of "I" and aversion to the world of "you." This is because you experience the world of "I" as something much closer and dearer to you and your life. These feelings of closeness and dearness to you cause you to develop a feeling of intimacy with the world around you with a sense of my cup, my table, and such, in the process of protecting the world of "I" from the world of "you." This is again because of your constant feeling of there being a threat to you from the world of "not-me" or "other." In other words, the world of "I" is always being threatened by the world of "you."

Ignorance is the root of all delusion. Attachment and aversion are the two most immediate afflictive emotions that directly arise from ignorance, not indirectly. Out of the three—ignorance, attachment, and aversion—there arise many other complex afflictive emotions or delusions. Primarily there are twenty-six afflictive emotions or delusions. These are the six root delusions and the twenty secondary delusions. The twenty secondary delusions are the symptoms or side effects of the six root delusions. For example, attachment is one of the six root delusions, whereas stinginess or miserliness is one of the secondary delusions and is a symptom of attachment. Pride is one of the six root delusions, whereas haughtiness, which is a symptom of pride, is one of the secondary delusions.

Ignorance, attachment, and aversion are called the three poisons of mind. Karma arises as a direct result of delusion. The three poisons of mind are the root of karma.

Ultimate Analysis: "Abiding in the Very Conclusion"

The total eradication or cessation of ignorance (the fundamental confusion between appearance and reality) along with its latent potency is known as liberation, *Moksha* or Nirvana.

Nirvana is a state of mind where ignorance is irreversibly eradicated. It is a state of everlasting peace and happiness. Nirvana is not an expensive physical place where someone can go if they can economically afford to buy a plane ticket. There is no physical means to reach the state of Nirvana.

The wisdom of emptiness conjoined with skillful means of the altruistic motivation—an impartial, unbiased and inclusive feeling of compassion—is the single means to reach the state of Nirvana. This can only be developed by the unified practice of Shamatha and Vipassana meditation. The unification of Shamatha and Vipassana focused on emptiness is fully gained upon reaching the first moment of the Path of Preparation/Linking. By reaching the Path of Preparation/Linking you are guaranteed the definite attainment of Nirvana without delay, without falling back or relapsing.

Vipassana meditation is an inner spiritual laser that removes your mental cataract and enables you to see the reality clearly as it is. Here I am using the term "mental cataract" as a metaphor for mental delusion. When you have a cataract in your eye, you do not see things clearly. Similarly, when you have a delusion in your mind, you do not see the reality clearly, as it is. You are seeing things in a distorted way, other than what they really are, just like when you see things as being very fuzzy and distorted when you have a cataract in your eye. Not seeing the reality of the world around you is the root cause for your samsaric pain, confusion, frustration, disappointment, and all other types of conflict between you and the rest of the world.

Before reaching the unification of Shamatha and Vipassana, you must cultivate them by alternating between single pointed concentration and analysis. As we examined in detail in chapter four, the cultivation of Shamatha is a manner of employing your mind to arise into an entity of single pointed awareness, a state with a sustained continuity, for a period of time. In this chapter, we will examine how the two meditative capacities of Shamatha and Vipassana enable us to focus and analyze so that we can test various views of reality, determine whether they are accurate and nondeceptive, and thus gain insight into the ultimate nature of all phenomena.

Vipassana Meditation

Vipassana meditation is a manner of applying non intellectual analysis within a single pointed frame of mind, and then abiding in the very conclusion of the analysis, whatever it may be.

Vipassana meditation, well grounded in Shamatha, will gradually or eventually eradicate the delusions from their root. By understanding this, you should strive for Shamatha first, and then seek to cultivate Vipassana.

Vipassana meditation, well grounded in Shamatha, is sufficient enough to erase the delusions from their root and refers to the meditative wisdom realizing emptiness and the subtle impermanence of any possible existing phenomenon. Soon, I will explain the proper cultivation of Vipassana, taking subtle impermanence and emptiness as its objects of focus—in other words, by using subtle impermanence and emptiness as the objects of analysis.

In order to cultivate Vipassana focused on subtle impermanence, you must have in the first place a good understanding of subtle impermanence. Without the understanding of subtle impermanence, the cultivation of Vipassana focused on subtle impermanence is not possible. Therefore I will now briefly explain subtle impermanence and emptiness on the intellectual level so that you the reader can understand these and begin to make them, when Shamatha is mastered, the subjects of Vipassana meditation. For a fuller treatment of emptiness, see the book *Two Subtle Realities: Impermanence and Emptiness*.

Ultimate Analysis: "Abiding in the Very Conclusion"

Levels of Understanding

There are three levels of understanding of subtle impermanence and emptiness. The first level of understanding is derived from learning, studying, and listening to teachings. This type of understanding is merely intellectual/conceptual and there is no definite certainty of ascertainment. The second level of understanding is derived not so much from learning and studying, but from your personal reflection, contemplation, and analysis. In this understanding there is a high degree of certainty of ascertainment. The third level of understanding is more experiential and it comes with the full definite certainty of ascertainment that one derives from meditation.

You must have at least the first level of understanding of subtle impermanence and emptiness in order to cultivate Vipassana focused on them.

Impermanence

In his *Exposition on Valid Cognition* (*Pramana-vartika*), Dharmakirti said: "Anything that has natural room to have a moment of stasis, that I define as permanent..." Since all conditioned things do not have room for a moment of stasis they are by nature impermanent.

Impermanence, or *anitya* in Sanskrit, means momentariness. Something that momentarily changes, even while carrying at least some of its characteristics from the first moment into the second moment, is impermanent. The momentariness of the object makes it impermanent, and momentariness exists within the object as its natural quality.

This momentary changing of the object is unpreventable by any external possible means and perpetual, constant change is inevitable due to the object's very nature.

There is no possible means to prevent it from changing. One mistakenly sees and grasps at the objects of pleasure and happiness as if they were permanent, while relating to them with the hope and expectation that they will last longer than they are able to by their nature. This is incredibly painful.

Normally in your naive mind you make everything permanent including your relationships and friendships with others, and then live your life with a belief in them as a permanent basis of pleasure and happiness. In reality, all of these relationships have the natural potential to change in the next moment without need of meeting with any external events or incidents. It is merely the cause that brought them into full existence that determines that change is inevitable. All phenomena are in the nature of constant change. The way a thing comes into being is as ever changing rather than as waiting to be changed.

Seeing what is not permanent as permanent reveals one of the most serious false perceptions that lie within you. This false perception can be erased by means of realizing the subtle impermanence of all possible existing phenomena, which are themselves produced by yet other ever changing, impermanent causes and conditions.

The impermanence or momentariness of an object is its state of constant change leading to its extinction without the requirement of it meeting with an external factor for its destruction. The object itself is naturally an entity of impermanence, not waiting to be ceased, extinguished or changed only upon meeting with an external circumstantial cause.

Anything that comes into being as a result of causes and conditions—all things do come into being as a result of causes and conditions—is impermanent due to being caused by other conditions, which are themselves impermanent. These things are ever changing and do not depend on some upcoming destructive factor to be momentary and impermanent. The very nature of everything as ever changing means that it lacks independent power or control to be able to exist in its second moment without moving towards it final extinction. Its extinction does not require any external factor because of the "way" it came into being rather than "what" it is going to be.

Ultimate Analysis: "Abiding in the Very Conclusion"

For example, in its first moment a pot exists as an entity that is not going to remain unchanged into its second moment. The natural ability of the pot to go out of its existence without depending on unexpectedly arising external destructive factors is the "way" in which the pot comes into existence. The pot comes into existence, like all objects, as impermanent. In each moment it is going out of existence. It comes into being as impermanent, as already going out of existence. The first moment of the pot coming into existence is already the moment where its extinction begins. The pot in its first moment is not going to remain unchanged into its second moment. That changeableness, momentariness, is the natural quality of the pot in its first moment. This excludes thinking that between the first and second moment of the pot something might change.

The pot comes into existence as momentary and impermanent, not waiting to be changed; nor is it waiting for its physical continuum to cease to exist upon meeting with any external circumstantial cause other than the cause that first brought it into existence. Rather it is the "how" and the "way" in which the pot is brought into existence that is important, which means the pot comes into existence not being static by its own nature.

The fact that the total extinction of the pot may occur upon meeting with an external destructive event is said to be the "gross" impermanence of the pot, and this type of realization is not useful to overcome from our fluctuating emotions. The realization of the pot that is not going to remain unchanged, while having no control of its own to exist in its second moment, is present within the way the pot comes into existence. This is said to be the most "subtle" impermanence of the pot, and realization of such impermanence is extremely useful.

The first cognizer that realizes this subtle impermanence of the pot is called the inferential cognizer (Sanskrit: *anumana-pramana*). An inferential cognizer is a conceptual mind, but is one of the most reliable minds. Why? Because such a conceptual mind deduces, with valid logic, the truth of reality, that whatever is being produced by causes and conditions by nature is imminent to go out of existence at any moment. This cannot be prevented by any means. The object has no self control to remain unchanged in the subsequent moment or in any subsequent moment.

So, whatever is being produced by causes and conditions is by nature impermanent, because it lacks control of its own to remain unchanged, and is proceeding toward its final extinction in every single moment. In other words, whatever is a product of causes and conditions must by nature be impermanent, and its total extinction is not dependent on any external secondary events. That things come into being as a result of impermanent, ever changing causes and conditions means that the things themselves are ever changing and impermanent. The way they come into being is as entities with ever changing nature, and not as entities waiting to be changed only upon meeting with external events that are not conducive for their continued existence.

The cause for the object's total extinction is within the cause that brought it into existence. For example, look at a candle: the wax and the wick are the two primary causes that bring the candle flame into existence. But the inevitable exhaustion of the wax and the wick itself is the cause for the extinction of the candle flame, which means that the total extinction of the candle flame is not dependent on any secondary external circumstances, such as someone blowing it out. Rather the cause that brought the candle flame into existence causes its extinction. Once the candle is lighted, the certainty of exhaustion of the wax and the wick is within the wax and the wick. Ever-changingness is their natural quality. It is their natural quality and no external means can prevent them from being exhausted. So, the cause for the total extinction of the candle flame is nothing other than the total exhaustion of the wax and wick. Awareness of the object's impermanent nature and its unpreventable disintegration from moment to moment is indeed extremely useful and prevents many emotional problems that cause pain and suffering.

An object's certainty of not remaining unchanged in its second moment because of its being produced by other ever-changing causes and conditions is subtle impermanence. The mere factor of the object's inability to remain unchanged in its second moment is the subtle impermanence of the object, say, a pot. These facts of the object prove that the objects are by nature impermanent and are not waiting to be impermanent after some time.

Reasoning for Full Understanding of Subtle Impermanence

Subtle impermanence is not easily perceived by ordinary beings. Moreover, it is a slightly obscure phenomenon that can be cognized or known through valid factual logic or reasoning. Here we will examine such reasoning in more detail.

There are three critical factors or three modes of reasoning within one logical analysis or statement directly leading to the arrival of the full understanding of subtle impermanence. This logical statement, also referred to as a syllogism, is called "conclusive reason of nature."

In general, you make many statements that are not based on conclusive reason. For example, imagine you pick from a mango tree ten mangoes that all have the same color. You eat one mango and it turns out to be sweet. The remaining nine mangoes are sitting in a basket on your dining room table. The next day one of your friends comes to see you and you two have a conversation about the mangoes. At the end you make a statement saying that, "Since the remaining nine mangoes are the same color, from the same tree, and the one I ate was sweet, then the rest are sweet as well." This statement is inconclusive, because you cannot prove the remaining nine mangoes are as sweet by positing that the one you ate was sweet as the reason for the other mangoes to be sweet in taste.

Any logical statement that does not have the "three modes of reasoning" is known as an inconclusive or incorrect reason. It is an inconclusive or incorrect reason because "that which is to be proven" cannot be proven in relation to the subject in a logical syllogism. For example, "sweet" is "that which is to be proven" in relation to the subject (the remaining nine mangoes) in a given logical syllogism. The syllogism can be established or constructed like this:

> The remaining nine mangoes are sweet because the one that I ate was sweet, and they are all from the same tree, and their colors match, therefore they must be sweet.

This type of logical syllogism does not have the "three modes of reasoning." In this syllogism the first mode of reasoning is not established because the posited reason (the one that I ate was sweet) is not present in the remaining nine mangoes. That means the remaining nine mangoes are not pervaded by the reason (sweet) given in the syllogism. In other words, all the remaining nine mangoes are not pervaded by the reason. The reason why they are not pervaded by the reason is that the possibility of some of the mangoes not being sweet is not fully negated from the mind of the person to whom the syllogism was constructed. The syllogism does not have the full logical force to remove the doubts (of some of the mangoes not being sweet) from the mind of the respondent, or *parabadin* in Sanskrit.

Any logical statement that has the "three modes of reasoning" is known as a conclusive or correct reason. Subtle impermanence can be initially realized or cognized on the basis of correct or conclusive reason of nature. Subtle impermanence is something that cannot be cognized directly without depending on a lengthy process of critical, logical analysis.

The logical statement of conclusive or correct reason of nature can be established or constructed like this:

The pot	**is impermanent**	**because it is a product.**
(subject)	(predicate)	(reason)

Ultimate Analysis: "Abiding in the Very Conclusion"

This conclusive reason of nature proves that the pot is impermanent through the force of the full establishment of the three modes of reasoning within the single logical syllogism. The three modes of reasoning are:

1. Property of the subject
2. Forward pervasion or subsequent pervasion
3. Counter pervasion

Repeating the syllogism, which will be explained below:

The pot	**is impermanent**	**because it is a product.**
(subject)	(predicate)	(reason)

The first mode of reasoning is called "property of the subject." What does this mean? It means the presence of the posited reason is in the subject and the subject must necessarily be pervaded by the reason. In the above logical syllogism, the pot is the subject. "Is a product" is the reason. In this case, being a product, which is the reason, is present in the pot, which is the subject. The pot is a product. Therefore, the subject pot is pervaded by being a product, which is the posited reason, in a given syllogism.

In other words, being a product must be the property of the pot, and whatever is a pot must be the product of other causes and conditions. All phenomena, including "pots," are products of ever changing causes and conditions.

The second mode of reasoning is called "forward or subsequent pervasion." What does this mean? The reason given in the logical syllogism must be pervaded/present only in the predicate, explicitly excluding the possible presence of the reason in the opposite phenomenon of the predicate, which is in this case "permanent." In this case "impermanent" is the predicate and as we know, "permanent" is the opposite of "impermanent." "Being a product" is the reason given in the logical syllogism. Forward pervasion is a mode of the pervasion of the predicate, which is impermanence by virtue of the reason, which is it being a product. Being a product of something naturally makes it impermanent and non-impermanent things cannot have the quality of being a product.

The third mode of reasoning is called "counter pervasion." What does it mean? It means that non impermanent (permanent) phenomena, which are the direct opposite phenomena of the predicate impermanent, are directly contradictory to impermanence, the predicate, and therefore must not be pervaded by the reason, which is product. Because of the subject pot being a product it cannot have the quality of permanence. And a permanent phenomenon cannot be the product of causes and conditions because something being a product and not being a product are directly contradictory to one another. Similarly, something being impermanent and permanent are directly contradictory to one another.

What is meant by directly contradictory? It means that the two existing things are contradictory with no possibility of something being both, as well as no possibility of something that can be neither. This means that every possible existing thing must be one or the other. There should not be something that can be neither. It must be one or the other, there being no third possibility.

Impermanence and permanence are directly contradictory to one another because every possible existing phenomenon must be either impermanent or permanent with no third possibility of something being neither.

Given below is the conclusion of the analysis of the three modes of reasoning:

1. The pot is a product.
2. Whatever is a product, without choice, must be ever changing or impermanent, and

Ultimate Analysis: "Abiding in the Very Conclusion"

3. Whatever is permanent with no choice must not be a product, and therefore must not be impermanent, because something being a product and not being a product are directly contradictory.

Likewise, something being impermanent and not being impermanent is again directly contradictory and will always be. The pot must be either impermanent or permanent. We know that the pot is a product. Therefore, the pot is impermanent because it is a product. Whatever is a product must by nature be impermanent. Whatever is not a product must not have the nature of impermanence.

Now the pot is fully established as impermanent by explicitly negating the false conception of the pot being permanent. Again, we know it is impermanent because it is a product of impermanent ever changing causes and conditions, like every other phenomenon.

Can there be a possible reason for an object not to be impermanent though it is produced by causes and conditions? If yes, then what is that reason? No reason can be found. This is one thing to consider and deeply ponder. Similarly, can there be a possible reason for an object not to be permanent when not being produced by causes and conditions? Again, no reason can be found. This is another thing to consider and deeply ponder. Can it be possible for an object to be neither impermanent nor permanent by nature? If yes, what could that object be, and what could be an example of this? What could be an example of an object that is neither impermanent nor permanent by nature? Upon finding the final answer to those three questions to be considered, only then can you establish the three modes of conclusive reasoning.

Once you have a good understanding of the three modes of reasoning, then your understanding of the subtle impermanence of the pot is certain to arise as an inferential cognition, the full ascertainment of subtle impermanence within your personal experience.

When you have arrived at the full ascertainment of subtle impermanence as a direct result of conclusive logical analysis, then you should simply rest or dwell in the subjective experience of subtle impermanence without doing any further analysis. This is said to be the proper cultivation of Vipassana meditation.

Emptiness

Now I will explain Vipassana meditation using Emptiness (Sanskrit: *shunyata*) as its object.

In order to meditate on emptiness you require clear intellectual or conceptual understanding of the true meaning of emptiness. Without this the meditator cannot have a clear picture of the object (emptiness) that is to be used as the object of meditation.

Emptiness is not a mere nothingness, nor nonexistence nor an empty space to be filled. Rather emptiness is the absence of inherent existence, or self evidence, or self sustainability. In brief, this means that no object or phenomenon has any fixed or rigid function so that it cannot interact with anything else or serve as something else with a different function. For example an object called table can be used as a seat and serve the function of a seat. In that moment, irrespective of whether you say I am sitting on my table or not, the object in reality serves your need for a seat and in that moment it exists as a seat with full functionality of being a seat in that moment, not a seat forever or permanently.

Inherent existence implies that an object exists on its own as self existent, self born, or existing by its own nature without depending on something other than itself. An example of something being inherently existent is something that can exist, for example, as a "table" without depending on something other than itself. Then, that "table" is said to be inherently existent. Another example would be the existence of something within the object "table" that dictates what that object will exist as no matter what the circumstances are. Any object that exists as a table on its own before you name it "table" for your need of that object as a table is said to be inherently existent.

Ultimate Analysis: "Abiding in the Very Conclusion"

In reality, there is not a single existing phenomenon that can either come into existence or exist on its own without depending upon something other than itself. Nothing does exist as a table, chair, or person before you name it table, chair, or person for your needs and necessity. Nothing exists as being more than the mere reference of the conventional name and term that you apply to it.

Things and events come into existence when they are given a name. They exist with only a subjective reality as having attractive or unattractive qualities, surely not with the real, objective and independent quality of making you happy or unhappy regardless of the state of your mind and attitude.

Things do not exist as a mere name or as more than a mere name. Seeing and believing in things as if they were a mere name is an extreme of nihilism, and seeing things as something more than the mere name is an extreme of absolutism or materialism.

However, things do not appear to your mind as a mere reference of conventional names and terms. Rather, things seem to be more than the mere name, and they appear to your mind as having, as if they had, inherent existence. They seem to exist from within themselves and on their own with an objective reality of attractiveness or unattractiveness, as being objects, which seem to be fully capable of making you happy or unhappy and they seem to serve as an objective source of happiness and unhappiness. This very false appearance of inherent existence becomes a basis for all sorts of grasping and clinging onto things and objects as being real in the way they appear.

Things do not exist in the way they appear to your mind. There is a gap or disparity between the way things and objects appear to you and the way they really are in their reality. An ordinary mind does not see this disparity, and constantly assents to the appearance of things rather than seeing the truth of reality. An ordinary mind assents to the appearance without inquiring. This is the fundamental problem of the ordinary mind, and you and everyone else are born with it from the beginning.

This problem cannot be dispelled or eradicated from your mindstream without gaining a full realization of emptiness (the lack of inherent existence in all things and objects, all phenomena), and being fully familiar with it. Without the proper experience of bringing the awareness of emptiness within every moment of perceptual interaction with every possible existing phenomenon, you cannot eradicate the false conception of things being inherently existent, nor can you eradicate the latent potency of this powerful misconception. Therefore, the wisdom realizing emptiness is said to be the single door to full liberation and Enlightenment.

In order to gain full realization of emptiness, you must have a complete understanding of the following four critical points. Each of them is a clear indication that every existing thing is empty of inherent existence. The four critical points are:

1. Interdependent origination
2. Mode of imputation
3. The way things normally appear to your mind
4. An object of negation, or that which is to be negated

Interdependent Origination

Emptiness must be understood within the context of the dependent and interdependent existence of things and events. Nothing can exist independently on its own without depending upon other factors that are not it, that are other than it. Nothing being able to exist as a table independently, on its own, is not proof that nothing can exist as a table. What it does prove is that nothing can have a pre-existing quality of table-ness that is fully capable to exist as a table on its own. However that thing or object has the power to generate the perception of that object as a table as a direct result of mere designation.

Ultimate Analysis: "Abiding in the Very Conclusion"

Every possible existing phenomenon, whether it be matter, mind, or energy, comes into being solely due to other factors that are not it, that are other than it. The mode of any thing or event—any possible object of the mind—coming into being is only possible through the means of something other than itself. All things and events have a dependent nature as their very existence and are therefore called "interdependently originating."

The word *pratityasamutpada* in Sanskrit is the same as the word *rten-drel* in Tibetan. The word *"rten"* means dependent. The word *"drel"* means relationship or connection. So, *rten-drel* means, dependent relationship or dependently arising.

Things and events do not exist independently outside their dependent relationship. Every phenomenon depends on something that is not it, that is other than it. For example, something cannot exist as a table independently from something that is not a table.

There are three dimensions of dependent origination. The first dimension is in terms of cause and effect. This means a causal dependence of existence, which means an effect is brought into existence due to various causes and conditions coming together to make the effect possible through their collective causal works. The effect is the final outcome of the subtle workings of causes and conditions. You must appreciate the intricate working mechanisms of causes and conditions in order to relate your life to the effect in a more productive way.

The second dimension of dependent origination is in terms of parts and whole. Nothing can exist as a whole without depending upon the parts coming together to make that whole. The parts that come together to form a whole are not the whole, and the whole, which appears from the collection of parts, is not any of the parts themselves. Nothing can be seen as a whole without the parts, and nothing can be seen as parts without the whole. Parts cannot exist independently from the whole, and the whole cannot exist independently from the parts. The whole and parts or fractions are dependent upon one another for their very existence.

The dependent relationship between the parts and the whole is not a causal relationship. Rather, it is a relationship of dependency to retain their continual identity of one being a part and the other being a whole. This dependent relationship to retain their continual entity indicates that they are empty of inherent existence due to the lack of any objective property to stand on their own.

The third dimension of interdependent origination is in terms of the imputation of the name/term. This is the subtlest form of dependent origination asserted by the Middle Way Buddhist School of Nagarjuna. So what is meant by imputation? Imputation means that nothing exists without depending on the names, terms, and labels that are imputed by the conventional mind of the designator. Whatever the designator designates, that term needs to be agreeable in the conventional world. For example, nothing can exist as a "table" without you first having the intention and need of that object as a table. Afterward, based on your need, you give it a label. Something that exists as a table is solely due to the force of the name "table" that you designate upon the object.

An object ceases to exist as a table the moment you detach or pull back the name "table" from where it was imputed. All the qualities of the table vanish with the name "table" once it is taken away. For instance, when a married man and woman have divorced, they no longer see one another as husband and wife. The reason for this is that the terms husband and wife have been disconnected or pulled back, and that causes the divorced man and woman no longer to see one another as husband and wife. This means that divorced man and woman no longer exist as husband and wife because the designated term "husband" and "wife" do not apply to the divorced couple.

Any thing or event—every phenomenon—exists only as a mere reference to the name, term, or label that is imputed upon the object by the conventional mind. Things do not exist separately from their imputed names and terms. However, things are not a mere empty name, without functional properties. Things are able to fulfill your conventional needs; therefore they do have functional properties. But when you search for their functional properties that fulfill your needs, you will not find them—neither the object nor its functional properties—as something existing objectively, as inherently existing. Not finding anything as something existing from the side of the object indicates that things and events do not exist as something more than a mere name either.

This subtle understanding of the total lack of objective property to stand on its own fully confirms that things and events are empty of inherent existence.

Mode of Imputation

The mode of imputation is a process of bringing something into conventional existence by giving it a conventional name. When you label an object with the name "table," you are giving that label to something that is not actually a table, since "table" is only a word or sound and your designation—and not the object itself. But the intent of giving the name "table" is to create an instant appearance of the name "table" merely by seeing the object upon which the name table is imputed.

The name "table" is called the imputed phenomenon or imputed object. The actual object upon which the name "table" is imputed is called the basis of imputation. The basis of imputation is a set of physical characteristics that have a certain shape, color, size, and texture, etc. or a series of instant moments of time and consciousness that is open to receive any possible conventional name, conceived by a conventional mind for its conventional need and fulfillment.

The imputed phenomenon or imputed object is not the basis of imputation, and the basis of imputation is not the imputed object. The as yet unnamed object is the basis of imputation. When that object is called "table" it becomes an imputed phenomenon. The purpose of imputation is not to cause the basis of imputation—the unnamed object—to become one with the object. The intent of imputation is to create an instant appearance of the imputed name as a direct result of seeing the basis of imputation.

When one imputes the name snake to a real snake and the name snake to a coiled rope, the mode of imputation is the same. In both cases, the name "snake" is imputed upon something that is not a snake in itself. There is no inherent snake-ness within either basis of imputation. But one exists as a snake and the other does not. This is because one serves as a basis for creating an instant appearance of the snake in the subsequent moment to a healthy and unconfused mind, whereas the coiled rope does not serve as a basis for creating an instant appearance of a snake in the subsequent moment. This means that you will not see the name "snake" in the rope whenever you see the rope. You will see the name "snake" in the real snake whenever you see its basis of imputation. Remember, the basis of imputation of the name "snake" is not a snake from within, but it is a base from which the appearances of the imputed snake arise with the functional properties of a snake, to a designator's conventional mind.

This understanding of the mode of imputation of all existing things and events—all existing objects—concludes that nothing can exist independently and objectively unless you label it as being table, chair, kitchen, David, friend, today, and so forth. Nothing can exist as a table unless you call it table for your need of it as a table.

The Way Things Normally Appear to Your Naive Mind

Normally things and objects appear to your mind in a different way than what they really are in reality. Although you may believe that your are reacting to something that is really there, you are actually reacting to something that is not there in the way you perceive it to be. Your reaction to the world around you is similar to the reaction of the person with the mistaken perception who reacts to the coiled rope as if it were a snake.

It is important to understand that things are appearing to your mind in five ways:

Ultimate Analysis: "Abiding in the Very Conclusion"

1. Things appear to your mind as existing from within themselves. They seem to be a self characterized entity.
2. Things appear to be locatable and findable somewhere within their parts or whole.
3. Things appear as being the imputed object or name whereas in reality they are nothing but a basis of imputation.
4. Things appear as being something more than the imputed name.
5. Things appear to your mind as existing on their own, with an objective quality of being able to make you happy or unhappy.

Every possible existing phenomenon appears to your mind in one or more of those five ways, but they do not actually exist in the way they appear. The five ways that things appear to your mind give you an instant impression or sense of them being inherently existent. This impression of inherent existence causes the development of a painful emotional response to something that does not exist outside its false appearance, just like the coiled rope appearing as a snake to a mistaken perception does not exist outside the false appearance of the rope.

Whether your emotional response is attachment or aversion, there is nothing out there that objectively can cause your emotional response. You become attached to an object, not because of what the object really is, but rather because of the way the object appears to you. Likewise you are repulsed by an object, again, not because of what the object really is, but rather, because of the way it appears to your mind.

This innate habit of painfully becoming attached or repulsed cannot be eradicated without fully realizing that things do not exist in the way they appear to your naive mind.

You must make an effort to understand how things normally appear to your mind and how you assent to the false appearance of the object as real. The realization of emptiness is not possible if you do not see a conflict or disparity between appearance and reality.

For example, objects appear to your mind with an objective quality of attractiveness that is capable of making you happy regardless of the state of your mind and attitude. However the object's attractive quality that seems to exist as part of the object will no longer be able to be found when your mind is not in a position or state to see it, and at that time the object is no longer capable of making you happy. The object's attractive or unattractive quality that is capable of making you happy or unhappy is a mere projection of your own mind, and certainly not due to the object's own power.

What it appears to be is not what it is in reality. You should be always mindful that there is a great discrepancy between something's appearance and the way it exists in reality. This mindful awareness of the disparity between appearance and reality will bring you closer to the understanding of emptiness of inherent existence. However, a true understanding of emptiness cannot arise without negating what is called the object of negation.

The Object of Negation

The object of negation is a misconception of inherent existence of things and events. It is a determined object of the mind that is grasping at any thing or event as truly existent, though inherent existence has never been part of the object's reality.

The false appearance of an object as truly, inherently existent is called the object of negation, or *gag-ja* in Tibetan. So, *gag-ja* refers to that which is to be negated in order to affirm or ascertain the true nature of existing phenomena—the true nature that is always hidden behind the false appearance to the ordinary dualistic mind.

For example, the true nature of the object "table," which is the emptiness of the table, is always hidden behind the false appearance of the table being truly, inherently existent. Another example: in the case of mistaking a rope for a snake, the reality of that object as a rope is very much obscured by the totally false appearance of the rope as a snake. The false appearance in this case is rope appearing as a snake. The way the rope appears as a snake and the object rope that is to be apprehended in reality contradict and thus there has occurred a discrepancy between the two—between appearance and the reality.

The understanding of the emptiness of the table cannot arise without negating the true inherent existence of the table. The emptiness of the table is nothing other than mere negation of the table's apparent inherent mode of existence, and without negating the inherent existence of the table one cannot see its emptiness.

In general, the true empty nature of any object is always covered or wrapped up or obscured by your conception or false perception of the object as existing inherently, for example as a table. It never occurs to your mind to question this and ask: "Do things really exist in the way they appear? Does the truth of the thing lie within its appearance? Does the way things appear to my mind match what they really are? Do the appearances of things and events give me the truth of what they are in reality?"

Perhaps up until today, you never questioned these things, and instead you directly assented to the false appearance of the object as truly existing, as existing inherently. You made what appears to your mind and how it appears as one. Therefore, in your mind how the object appears to you mistakenly becomes one with what the object really is. This misperception and this assenting to appearances are what prevent you from seeing emptiness. This misconception cannot be removed from your mind or psyche without realizing emptiness through negating the object of negation.

The object of negation, or *gag-ja*, is a combination of two things: (1) It is a quality (inherent existence) that is being projected on the object by your mind, and (2) it is the object's false appearance of being that projected quality. In other words, the object appears as if it exists with the imputed or projected quality (inherent existence) as its inherent nature.

When you put the name "table" upon something, only then does that object exist as a table for you. But whenever the object, upon which you put a name of table, appears to you, it will never appear as a table merely because you named it "table." Rather it appears to you as being a table from its own side by giving you an impression of table-ness.

Table-ness here means a quality of the object that is capable of giving rise to a perception of that object as a table, no matter who sees it, by preventing any possibility that anyone could see it as a non-table.

In reality, an object that you see as a table will not prevent someone else from seeing and using it as a chair. For example, the water which you see as something to drink, does not have any quality that prevents a fish from seeing it as something to live in. In brief, things do not have any objective reality, such as table-ness, chair-ness, or water-ness, apart from the subjective reality imparted by, given by, names and terms that have a temporary meaning and purpose.

Nothing can exist as a table inherently. Nothing can cause a perception of any object as a table or force using it as a table at any and all times and in any and all circumstances. Rather the perceiver of the object misperceives that object as inherently existent, as having table-ness. In reality the object has no inherent functionality or any other inherent quality.

Similarly, nothing can exist as inherently attractive from its own nature by causing or forcing a perception of it as attractive at any time, in any geographical location of the world, in any human society, and in any circumstance. For example, every human society as well as individuals have different standards of beauty and what is attractive. In Eastern culture someone with light skin and a slightly plump body is considered to be attractive and beautiful. In Western culture often someone with a thin, tall body, with darker, tanned skin is considered more attractive and appealing. So, there is no inherent universal standard of beauty, but instead, each individual's ideas and beliefs of something possessing beauty and attractiveness are equally correct.

Ultimate Analysis: "Abiding in the Very Conclusion"

An Easterner's perception of a person with light skin and having a slightly plump body as attractive and appealing is correct. But because this is correct does not mean that the person with light skin and a slightly plump body is a universal standard of beauty or has any inherent quality of beauty. If this were so, then a Westerner's perception too must see that person as attractive and appealing to them.

A Westerner's perception of someone with a thin, tall body with darker skin as attractive and appealing is also correct and a valid perception. Again, correct and valid does not mean that a person with a thin and tall body with darker skin is a universal standard of beauty. If this were so, then an Easterner's perception too must see it as attractive and appealing to them.

The ideas of attractiveness and unattractiveness are merely a perceptually measured quality that is imposed on the external object, event, or person rather than an inherent, self presented quality of attractiveness and unattractiveness.

The mind grasping at things as if they had an objective quality of attractiveness and unattractiveness is invalid. Such grasping is the seed of painful emotional experiences of attachment, desire, lust, fear, anger, repulsion, and conflict. Living a life that is constantly making the world around you either an object of attachment or repulsion, or one of indifference, is something that you really don't want to live with.

The universal solution for this painful cycle of samsaric existence is the proper cultivation of meditative awareness of emptiness—what is called Vipassana-Bhavana.

Vipassana-Bhavana, or Insight Meditation that is single pointedly focused on emptiness, is directly contradictory to the mind grasping onto things as inherently existent with an inherently attractive or unattractive quality. This meditative awareness of emptiness directly invalidates the mind grasping onto things as inherently existent. This is because the ascertainment of things as being empty of inherent existence and the ascertainment of things as being inherently existent are directly contradictory to one another. The two ideas or perceptions cannot exist simultaneously. One cannot exist due to the force of presence of the other.

In this case, the mind grasping at things as inherently existent cannot exist or manifest in your mindstream due to the force of the presence of awareness of things being empty of inherent existence, just as you can't hold the directly contradictory thoughts of "this object is black" and "this same object is white" at the same time.

The mind that is grasping onto things as inherently existent and the mind seeing things as empty of inherent existence are totally opposite to each other. The mind grasping onto things as inherently existent is incorrect, wrong, and invalid, whereas the mind seeing things as being empty of inherent existence is correct and valid. One view ascertains the reality and the other does not. One has a correct logical base that does not contradict ultimate analysis, and the other does not have a correct logical base and does contradict ultimate analysis.

The Ultimate Analysis

Ultimate analysis is a type of nonintellectual analysis that is in search of the ultimate truth of any possible existing phenomena. It is called nonintellectual because it is not motivated by an interest to learn something without giving up your ideas and concepts of what you are searching for through analysis. Rather, you are analytically searching for the ultimate truth by yourself, ready to surrender to the truth of reality without mulling over your own ideas and concepts of what you normally think of as reality.

Nonintellectual analysis that is employed as a key element of Vipassana meditation is not based on your idea and concept of finding what you are searching for. It is purely based on a conclusive logical reason that has nothing to do with your ideas and concepts. In other words, it is a logically based search for reality rather than idea based search for reality.

Ultimate Analysis: "Abiding in the Very Conclusion"

The most prominent logically based analysis is called fourfold analysis and was originally taught by Nagarjuna, and later elaborated by his disciple, Chandrakirti, as what is known as sevenfold analysis. Here, I am not going to discuss those two types of analysis in detail in order to avoid causing confusion in the reader's mind. Instead, since emptiness should be understood and is best understood within the context of interdependent arising, I will explain the nonintellectual analysis that should be employed on the basis of logical reason known as the "king of interdependent arising reasoning."

The great Indian master Nagarjuna said in his book *Ratnamala* or *The Precious Garland*:

> Whatever is dependently originated,
> I call that to be empty.
> And that too is dependently designated,
> And this is the middle way.

Similarly he stated in his book known as *Mulamadhyamaka-Karika* or *The Root of Wisdom*:

> There is no phenomenon,
> That is not dependently arising.
> Therefore, there is no phenomenon,
> That is not empty (of inherent existence).

These two verses explicitly indicate that emptiness should be understood within the context of the principle of interdependent arising. Emptiness is not to be equated with mere nothingness. It is a mere lack of self existence or a mere absence of inherent, independent existence. Emptiness in terms of dependent arising is the subtlest and most complete form of emptiness that was originally taught by the Buddha and later revealed by Nagarjuna with his detailed and elaborate explanation.

An idea or understanding of emptiness that is not rooted in the principle of the dependently arising nature of all phenomena is surely not a correct understanding of emptiness. This mistaken idea or understanding of emptiness—an idea of emptiness not based on the interdependent arising of all phenomena—certainly has an element of nihilism as well as a denial of the conventional reality. As said by Acharya Aryadeva:

When the emptiness is wrongly understood,
A person with little intellect will be destroyed.
When the poisonous snake is unskillfully seized
You are left in pain from being bitten.

You must have complete identification of the object of negation in order to see the image of emptiness, the absence of inherent existence. Initially you will see emptiness as nothing other than the mere experience of "not finding the searched for object" in the way it normally appears to your mind, and also not finding the searched for object as something other than the way it appears. You have lost the object temporarily by leaving the searching mind with a mere experience of not finding or of losing the one thing that you are searching for.

Not finding anything that can be seen as, for example, "table" by breaking every single part of the table saying that this is not a table and this is also not a table, itself is not the meaning of the emptiness of the table, though it does leave the mind with a sense of emptiness or vacuity. This is nothing other than the deconstruction/destruction of the conventional existence of the table, and surely is not the deconstruction of the inherent existence of the table. Therefore, the experience of not finding a table after breaking down its parts and saying that those are not the table is not the understanding of the emptiness of the table.

The complete and unmistaken understanding of emptiness must arise by the force of the total deconstruction of the inherent existence of things and events. The inherent existence of things is neither a physical object nor something that exists on the object like rust on iron. It is not something to be removed or pulled out from the things and events like rust being removed from rusty iron.

Inherent existence is a false mode of existence of things and events that is conceived within your own mind, and then superimposed on external existing phenomena. Your whole life experience until now is based on your false perception that this is the mode of existence of the world around you, and your habit of seeing it and all objects with an inherent quality is deeply rooted in your mindstream.

So far you are not aware of this whole process of your mind conceiving or assuming the inherent mode of existence and superimposing it on external objects. Rather, you are deeply convinced that things and events are coming into existence with that mode of inherentness.

Not knowing of this entire process that naturally occurs in every single moment of your perceptual interaction with the world is known as "fundamental ignorance" or "confusion." It is the most subtle cognitive flaw that acts as the root of all delusion (Sanskrit: *klesha*). Here again I would like to make sure that you understand the meaning of delusion in this context. Delusion does not mean a breakdown from conventional reality, but delusion means highly distorted thoughts and emotions that instantly create turmoil in our state of mind and influence our actions inevitably to be negative with undesirable consequences. In Buddhism, this confusion is said to be the prime cause for the existence of samsara characterized by pain and suffering that cannot be avoided once you are born in samsara, are plunged into samsara.

The correct and complete understanding of emptiness takes place or arises from the point where the inherent mode of existence of things and events ceases to appear to you, or is fully negated, while the functionality of things and objects is intact along with their quality of fulfilling your conventional needs.

At the beginning when you realize emptiness while meditating, the appearance of the object that is being realized as empty will cease, together with the inherent mode of existence of the object. The object itself will disappear. However, the appearance of the object will return to your perception in a different way, with a different affect, when you arise from meditation and the experience of its emptiness.

The understanding of emptiness should cause you to see a change in the mode of appearance of the object rather than causing you to see change in its conventionality as far as functioning to meet your needs. At stake is the true appearance of the object, which true appearance replaces the previous false appearance of the object as being inherently existent.

The Madhyamika School's conclusive reason known as "the king of dependent arising reasoning" leaves you with no other choice than to reach the full ascertainment of emptiness. The "king of dependent arising reasoning" can be constructed like this:

The table	**lacks inherent existence**	**because of being dependently originated**
(subject)	(predicate)	(reason)

This logical statement primarily makes three conclusive points. Each conclusive point makes it impossible to determine that the table is not empty. It is impossible to determine that the table exists inherently, by its own power. The three conclusive points are:

1. Whatever arises in dependence on something other than itself does not exist inherently (from its own nature). The subject "table" does not exist inherently because it is dependently originated.

2. Whatever arises inherently, from its own nature, must not be dependent upon something other than itself.

3. Whatever arises in dependence upon something other than itself must lack self existence or independent existence. And whatever arises inherently from its own nature must not have the dependent nature for its existence.

Ultimate Analysis: "Abiding in the Very Conclusion"

Something that exists independently or inherently and something that exists dependently with non self representational qualities are directly contradictory to one another without there being a third possibility. Having no third possibility means that every possible existing phenomenon must be either one or the other. There is no other possibility that something can be both, nor can it be neither. In other words, there is no room for something that can be both nor is there any possibility that something cannot be either.

Finally you will arrive at the full conclusion/confirmation that the object "table" is empty of inherent or independent existence. All doubts as well as any possible room in which the object "table" can exist with a mode of inherent existence, without being dependent upon something other than itself, are completely dispelled.

When you employ analysis through the method of the Madhyamika reason, you will fail to find the searched for object in the way it normally appears to your mind, or in the way you normally think of it to be—that is as being inherently existent. This not finding of the object confirms that the inherently existent object is unfindable after ultimate analysis. The unfindability or unfindableness of the inherently existent object is called emptiness.

The unfindability of the inherently existing object does not mean that the object is nonexistent. What it does mean is that it does not exist in the way it appears or has always before appeared to exist to your dualistic mind.

In brief, whatever comes into being in dependence upon something other than itself does not have room to exist on its own, and this must confirm that it is empty of inherent existence, and that it has no independent existence.

This mere absence of inherent existence, this lack of objective meaning, is said to be emptiness. Unless there is a name imputed upon the object, the object itself has no meaning. It is the imputed name that gives meaning to the object.

At the beginning, when you experience emptiness fully, it will not be anything other than the mere shocking experience of finding that what you normally thought of as "something always out there with objective reality" has never existed at all. This shocking experience will push you away from resting/dwelling in emptiness, and your experience of emptiness will be too short and too fragile. Your experience of emptiness will be like seeing some very precious object under the flash of lightning but failing to hold it for further use.

This explains that the mere intellectual understanding of emptiness itself is not really useful unless you painfully strive for the meditative experience of emptiness on the basis of correct intellectual or inferential understanding of emptiness. This can be done only by perfecting Shamatha and then employing Vipassana.

Meditative experience of emptiness will have sufficient enough force to damage or puncture the mind that is grasping at the concept of inherent existence even when you are in post meditative life experience in relation to normal conventional appearance.

Through the force of nonintellectual analysis relying on the method of Madhyamika reason, you will arrive at its conclusion with a deep nonthinking experience of the total loss of the searched for object, namely the inherent existence of the phenomenon you are looking at. You must train yourself how to rest or be there as one with the subjective experience of the loss of the object without questioning it the moment you arrive at this experience. You must learn how to remain with it without making an effort either to go further or to pull back.

However, you will surely make at least one of five errors in the beginning, which will corrupt the subjective experience of emptiness. In other words, the error pulls you away from the deep experience of emptiness. The five errors you might make are:

1. Making an effort to affirm or acknowledge with a feeling of "wow."
2. Emotional fear of losing the particular phenomenon or object you are looking at. The kind of feeling like, "I may lose it."

Ultimate Analysis: "Abiding in the Very Conclusion"

3. Anticipation, a feeling of what will come in the next moment.
4. Curiosity, an effort to see what it really looks like, what the object that is not after all inherently existent looks like.
5. Making effort to translate emptiness itself or your subjective experience of emptiness into human language or words.

You must train not to make any of those errors when you are meditating on emptiness. In fact, there is nothing to be affirmed or to be negated in the subjective experience of emptiness. It is a nonthinking experience of mere emptiness or vacuity where there are no boundary, no conceptual recognizable phenomena, no shape, no color, no location, no time, no increase, no decay, no memory, no beneficiary, no winner, no loser, and neither relation nor non relation.

When you are meditating on emptiness, you are not just using emptiness as a focal object, but rather you are emphasizing more the mode of maintaining the strength of the subjective experience of emptiness. Therefore, it is extremely important to keep checking on the quality of the subjective experience of emptiness from time to time while you are meditating on emptiness to see whether the subjective experience of emptiness is still there or if you have lost it.

It is very possible that you will lose the actual subjective experience of emptiness after meditating for ten to fifteen minutes, and you will be resting or sitting in a total blank state of mind.

When you have lost the strength of the subjective experience of emptiness, you must once again go through the process of analysis until you regain the maximum strength of the subjective experience of emptiness. And then, once again, simply rest in it by sustaining the force of the subjective experience of emptiness without doing further analysis. This repeated meditational practice of alternating analysis and concentration on emptiness eventually leads to the unification of Shamatha and Vipassana.

The union of Shamatha and Vipassana focused on emptiness is fully attained when you reach the point where one single act of analysis on emptiness induces an effortless concentration on emptiness at the end of that one analysis. When you attain the union of Shamatha and Vipassana, there is a complementary balance between analysis and concentration within the continuum of the same meditative mind.

The meditative practice of alternating analysis and concentration on emptiness, over a long period of time, brings you deeper comfort in resting in the subjective experience of emptiness. This is the way you should enhance and deepen your understanding of emptiness. Through this training, you eventually arrive at an understanding of emptiness that is direct, intuitive, and non conceptual. You will gain the direct, intuitive, and non conceptual understanding of emptiness only upon reaching the Path of Seeing, which is described below.

The first moment of the direct realization of emptiness serves as the direct antidote to all one hundred and twelve delusions that are stemming from the conceptual grasping at the inherent existence of things and events.

“ You attain Enlightenment only through sequentially training in the five Paths and ten Bhumis, employing meditation at every step. ”

7

The Road Map of the Paths and Bhumis

THE FIVE PATHS AND ten Bhumis offer a detailed road map to Enlightenment for spiritual travelers. They explain in detail the various characteristics and necessary conditions for spiritual progress, starting from the beginning and progressing into higher stages. The reason why I would like to give a concise introduction to the Paths and Bhumis in conjunction with meditation instruction is that the ultimate purpose of meditation is to attain a state of Enlightenment. To train in the Paths and Bhumis, mastery of both Shamatha meditation and Vipassana meditation is indispensable. The way to attain Enlightenment is by advancing the purity and perfection of ethics (*shila*), meditation (*bhavana*) and wisdom (*prajna*). You advance the purity and perfection of these three by following the five Paths and achieving the ten Bhumis. You make progress gradually step by step until you fully attain Enlightenment.

This chapter contains advanced teachings. If you find the material difficult, do not take this as a source of discouragement or lose interest. Rather, through the force of studying, contemplating, and meditating, you will plant the seeds for future understanding.

As I have said, mastery of both Shamatha and Vipassana meditation is the indispensable requirement for training in the Paths and Bhumis and progressing toward Enlightenment. You move sequentially through the steps or stages and on a certain stage, employing both Shamatha and Vipassana, you eliminate a specific delusion and attain a specific realization upon the elimination of that specific delusion. The stages that you move through are called the Paths. The stage where you eliminate a particular delusion and then gain a specific realization as a result of eliminating that delusion is called a Bhumi. The five Paths are:

1. Path of Accumulation
2. Path of Preparation or Linking
3. Path of Seeing or Insight
4. Path of Meditation or Familiarization
5. Path of No More Learning or Beyond Training

It is on the third Path, the Path of Seeing or Insight, and the fourth Path, the Path of Meditation or Familiarization, that you train the ten Bhumis. The five Paths are indicated by these words of the Prajnaparamita mantra—"the mother of wisdom"—found in the *Heart Sutra*: GATE GATE PARAGATE PARASAMGATE BODHI SVAHA (which means "Gone, Gone, Gone Beyond, Thoroughly Gone Beyond, Be Established in Enlightenment").

The first and second Gate refer to the first two of the five Paths, the Path of Accumulation and the Path of Preparation. Paragate refers to the third Path, the Path of Seeing and indicates passing beyond the conceptual or intellectual level into the non conceptual level in which dualistic appearance first vanishes, at least briefly. The practitioner on the first Bhumi, who has just gained the perception of emptiness, has a momentary experience of non duality. But duality is only momentarily suppressed at the first Bhumi. It is not permanently eradicated until the tenth Bhumi. From the tenth Bhumi the deceptive appearance will never again occur. Parasamgate refers to the Path of Meditation or Familiarization, during which by alternating Shamatha and Vipassana you familiarize yourself again and again with emptiness, which you have just directly glimpsed or seen on the Path of Seeing. Through repeated meditation on emptiness, you finally reach beyond cyclic existence, or unenlightened existence, to the level of the enlightened state. Therefore, Bodhi Svaha refers to the fifth Path, the Path of No More Learning or Beyond Training.

The meditator travels through Paths and Bhumis by combining method and wisdom. Method refers to 1) Great Compassion, 2) Bodhicitta, and 3) the unselfish activities of giving, ethics, patience, and other paramitas. Wisdom primarily refers to the realization of emptiness (*shunyata*), including subtle impermanence (*anitta*) and selflessness (*anatma*), and the unsatisfactory nature of samsaric existence as it is experienced by those lacking wisdom.

The five Paths and ten Bhumis are an internal process. Path, or *marga* in Sanskrit, means a realizing mind in which there is an active function of compassion and wisdom realizing emptiness or subtle impermanence. Those two—compassion and wisdom realizing emptiness—are advancing along together on the five Paths to become increasingly merged and united or infused with one another, thus gaining a force or power for the elimination of a particular or specific delusion. As the specific delusion is eliminated, you gain a new and fresh realization that enables you the practitioner to draw closer to attaining Enlightenment.

Bhumi is a Sanskrit word that means ground or level. It is called a ground or Bhumi because within it special spiritual qualities are engendered that act as the antidote to specific delusions. For example, on the first level, or first Bhumi, the one hundred and twelve delusions, that stem from aversion or attachment (ultimately from ignorance) and are conceptually fabricated distorted thoughts and emotions, are eradicated because of the antidote (the first moment of the direct realization of emptiness). An antidote is the method or opposing force that eliminates what is to be eliminated and makes it impossible for what was eliminated to return in the subsequent moment. There are a total of ten levels or Bhumis that are within the Path of Seeing and the Path of Meditation. These Bhumis are also called the ten Bodhisattva levels.

The five Paths, ten Bhumis, and their main attainments and cessations are as follows:

Paths	Bhumis	Attainments & Cessations
Path of Accumulation		Unfabricated or spontaneous arising of Bodhicitta
Path of Preparation / Linking		Conceptual union of Shamatha and Vipassana Meditative experience of emptiness, though still conceptual, is approaching a non conceptual, direct, intuitive experience
Path of Seeing	1. Very Joyous	Direct, non conceptual experience of emptiness; elimination of 112 acquired delusions; perfection of generosity
Path of Meditation	2. Stainless 3. Luminous 4. Radiant 5. Difficult to Overcome 6. Approaching 7. Gone Afar 8. Immovable 9. Excellent Intelligence 10. Cloud of Dharma	Progressive elimination of 1. obstruction of innate delusions 2. obstruction to omniscience or Enlightenment Perfection of the remaining paramitas
Path of No More Learning		Buddhahood; full release from all obscurations to Enlightenment; perfection of all attainments Permanent unification of meditative and post meditative awareness perceiving simultaneously the two truths—ultimate truth of emptiness and conventional truth of appearance

The Road Map of the Paths and Bhumis

I have said that as you make progress toward Enlightenment, you move through the five Paths and ten Bhumis. In each stage, purely intellectual/conceptual understanding gives way more and more to experiential understanding, as this experiential understanding progressively deepens. Your practice moves from Path to Path through a non-meditative experience of life to a meditative experience of life. A non-meditative experience is daily life, any experience that occurs when you are not engaged in meditation. This is the time when you experience conventional reality as dualistic, when your five senses are actively engaged.

When you move to meditative experience, your five senses stop engaging you and the appearances of conventional reality cease to function. What is left behind is a mere state of vacuity or emptiness. Once conventional reality stops, temporarily, a pure state of vacuity is left. The meditator abides there without negating or affirming. That we call the meditative experience.

The non-meditative experience is all conceptual, intellectual. When you go deeper, the meditative experience is experiential, and your understanding of emptiness moves from an intellectual understanding to an experiential understanding.

There are two main types of obscurations or obstructions to overcome on the road to Enlightenment: the obstruction to Nirvana or liberation and the obstruction to Enlightenment or omniscience.

Individual liberation (Nirvana) means you have achieved complete cessation of manifested delusions or emotions. You have totally eradicated ignorance (the fundamental confusion between appearance and reality) along with its latent potency. For practitioners who aim for their own spiritual interests or well-being Nirvana or Moksha is enough. But individual liberation is not enough for practitioners on the Mahayana Path to Enlightenment. They are not satisfied with attaining individual liberation but are looking for more than that. With individual liberation, although the manifested emotions or delusions are ended, a subtle residue is left behind in the mindstream. This disturbs and interferes with helping others. Those who wish to be of greatest benefit in alleviating suffering for all sentient beings therefore strive for Enlightenment—a state of mind that is fully perfected.

As I said, on the Mahayana Path to Enlightenment there are two sets of obscurations that need to be eradicated, the obstruction to Nirvana and the obstruction to Enlightenment. The obstruction to Nirvana is the "afflictive" obscurations. The obstruction to Enlightenment is the "cognitive" obscuration. Afflictive or emotional obscurations are disturbing emotions and attitudes which prevent Liberation. The cognitive obscuration prevents omniscience (Enlightenment). Furthermore, obscurations may be innate or learned/acquired. Innate obscurations have been on the mindstreams of ordinary beings in samsara since beginningless time. They stay with us from rebirth to rebirth. Acquired obscurations are learned in each lifetime as we take on mistaken beliefs.

All afflictive emotions, thoughts, and their latent potentials that are themselves ready to manifest into afflictive emotions upon meeting with external provoking circumstances, are said to be obscurations to Liberation. For example the latent potential of anger lies in your mind. When you are exposed to an external unpleasant situation or provocation, that latent potential of anger manifests into an active state of anger.

The latent potential of afflictive emotions manifests in thoughts and emotions and then these motivate you to do negative actions of body, speech and mind and thus create negative karma. This latent potential of afflictive emotions is neither consciousness nor matter, nor energy with a physical origin. It is not matter because it can turn into consciousness. Something that is not in the nature of consciousness cannot turn into consciousness. Nor is this latent potential of afflictive emotions consciousness, because it is in a latent or dormant state. In Buddhism whatever is consciousness should be active, not dormant. Whatever is time should be present time. Whatever is a person should be a living person. There is no such thing as a dead person. Therefore Dharmakirti said "Everybody dies, but no one is dead yet."

The subtlest residual imprint of the mind that grasps at the inherent existence of things and events (including the self) is said to be the obstruction to omniscience or Enlightenment. This subtle imprint is also said to be the cognitive obscuration. After Nirvana but before Enlightenment this subtle imprint can never turn into afflictive emotion or thought but is only a trigger. For example, you have a habit of smoking or drinking. That habit is more or less like a latent force that initiates for you to drink or to smoke. That latent force is the trigger or motivating force. The latent habit never turns into the actual act of drinking or smoking. Habit is some kind of built force that triggers you wanting to repeat the habitual act. That habit or force is not the action of smoking. It only initiates, motivates, instigates, and triggers you to want to repeat that act over and over again.

As I just said, after one attains Nirvana these subtle residual imprints themselves cannot manifest or arise as afflictive emotions, nor can they arise in a mind grasping at inherent existence. But they do give rise to an instantaneous sense of things and events as being inherently existent, and although this is a delusion that cannot lead to negative actions and negative karmic seeds, it causes a very slight delay in response. The response of a fully enlightened being to any event or situation is not delayed.

As you progress along the Paths and achieve the Bhumis one by one your realization becomes more and more refined and stable. You slowly approach Enlightenment.

The problem or delusion of having a sense of things and objects as inherently real weakens increasingly on the Paths but can be finally or completely eradicated only by the vajra like meditative equipoise belonging to the very last moment of the tenth Bhumi, which is on the Path of Meditation, the fourth of the five Paths. From then on, the meditator remains in a meditative state while carrying on the unselfish enlightened activities in everyday life, and interacting with the conventional world of deceptive appearances.

This non dual, permanent unification of meditation and post meditation in which there is nothing left that needs to be realized, and nothing left that needs to be eradicated or corrected, is called

Enlightenment. In other words, it is the highest trained awareness in which there is neither increase nor decrease. It is a blissful non thinking and omniscient all knowing mind that does not leave a memory trace behind it. The omniscient mind is always dwelling in the present and there is no role for memory.

Omniscience or Enlightenment is the highest spiritual attainment, and the process of training for its attainment is very gradual and slow. You can attain Enlightenment only through sequentially training in the five Paths and ten Bhumis, employing meditation at every step.

Path of Accumulation

The first of the five Paths is called Accumulation because it is the first stage on which begins the actual accumulation of merit that carries the potential for all of your practice and Dharma understanding to become an actual cause for the attainment of Enlightenment. Once you are training on the first Path, it's just a matter of time before you enter into the second Path. The Path of Accumulation is fully attained the moment you have gained the unfabricated or spontaneous arising of Bodhicitta for the very first time. Once you have gained this you have fully arrived at the gate of the second Path, the Path of Preparation.

On the Path of Accumulation, your understanding of emptiness is very limited. It is conceptual and intellectual, and has just a little meditative taste of emptiness. The practice of Shamatha and Vipassana focused on emptiness has not yet conjoined in complementary work, and analysis is absent in terms of you the meditator. You are unable to carry out further analysis because you are in the post analytic concentrated state of the experience of emptiness. Having used analysis in Vipassana meditation to arrive at an understanding or taste of emptiness, you cannot immediately analyze further at that moment. You cannot dwell in your glimpse of emptiness and deepen it through continuing Vipassana right away. Your mind is still grasping at the inherent existence of things although it has the beginning of the understanding that the appearance is false. The mind grasping at the inherent existence of things and objects, as well as the delusive thoughts and emotions stemming from the grasping mind have not yet begun diminishing in strength. However, your understanding of emptiness, subtle impermanence, and other such concepts is gaining strength within each moment as you move toward the second Path, the Path of Preparation.

Attaining the first Path, the Path of Accumulation, does not guarantee the attainment of Enlightenment. Indeed, if you have attained the Path of Accumulation you can fall back or relapse into rebirths in the lower realms of existence that seriously delay your spiritual journey towards Enlightenment. Even when you attain the Path of Accumulation, you still have the karmic potential together with the full force of persistent afflictive emotions and thoughts that are essential for the karmic seeds to bring their negative results and possibly propel you to a lower rebirth.

Path of Preparation or Linking

You have attained the second of the five Paths, the Path of Preparation, when you reach the point where Shamatha and Vipassana focused on emptiness are united and the complementary work between concentration and analysis is fully present. Before this, you have had to alternate Shamatha and Vipassana, but now on the Path of Preparation they are conjoined. On this stage, you have a high degree of meditative experience of both emptiness and subtle impermanence that have gained the strength for weakening the force of delusion.

This second Path is called Preparation or Linking because it is this stage from which the actual effort that strengthens the wisdom realizing emptiness begins in full force, by substantially decreasing the conceptual element of emptiness. This effort for strengthening the wisdom realizing emptiness is called Preparation.

The Path of Preparation has four sequential levels. The reason for this is because the meditative experience of emptiness increases in four phases within the Path of Preparation. These levels are named 1) heat, 2) peak, 3) forbearance and 4) supramundane.

During each level, the meditative experience of emptiness itself not only increases and intensifies, but the meditator finds new, fresh, and increased comfort in the confidence he or she is gaining in the act of dwelling in emptiness. In each level, the meditative experience of emptiness, which is still largely conceptual, is getting closer and closer to turning into a wholly non conceptual, direct, and intuitive experience. The meditator's experience of emptiness becomes stronger and more stable, while the less conceptual opposite force of the experience of emptiness (namely seeing or misperceiving the inherent existence of objects) is diminishing during an uninterrupted process.

The meditator who is in the fourth level of the Path of Preparation ("supramundane") moves from a still partly conceptual understanding of emptiness into a wholly non conceptual, direct, experiential, and intuitive understanding of emptiness. At this point, one enters the Path of Seeing.

Path of Seeing and the First Bhumi

The Bhumis begin on the third Path, the Path of Seeing, and end at the very last moment of the fourth Path, the Path of Meditation. The first Bhumi belongs to the Path of Seeing and the remaining nine belong to the Path of Meditation. In other words, the Path of Seeing has one Bhumi or level.

You have reached the third Path, the Path of Seeing, and the first Bhumi when your conceptual understanding of emptiness turns into a non conceptual, direct and intuitive experience.

The third Path is called Seeing because it is the level at which the meditator experiences emptiness in a different way than he or she has ever experienced it before. Up until now, the meditator has experienced or understood emptiness in an objective form with a sense of perceiving it. That is, emptiness is seen as an object of the mind with inherent existence. Before this point the deepest understanding of emptiness has not yet become wholly a part of your being. But on the Path of Seeing, you experience or understand emptiness in a subjective form without a sense of seeing emptiness objectively and as inherently existent, and the understanding of emptiness has now become a part of your being, of who you are.

The first moment of the direct realization of emptiness on the Path of Seeing serves as a direct antidote to the one hundred and twelve acquired/learned afflictive delusions and the conceptually formed grasping at self. The one hundred and twelve delusions stem from aversion and attachment, which themselves stem from ignorance and are conceptually fabricated distorted thoughts and emotions (Tibetan: *nyon-mong kuntag*). The direct realization of emptiness on the Path of Seeing occurs in a state of meditative equipoise. Meditative equipoise is wisdom in single pointed concentration on emptiness, in the process of directly eliminating or of having already eliminated the mind's own respective object of abandonment, which is the one hundred and twelve delusions that are exclusively conceptually constructed or formed delusions. The primary objects of abandonment on the Path of Seeing are the one hundred and twelve acquired/learned afflictive delusions together with their root of the conceptually formed misconception of self.

The first moment of meditative equipoise, which is an active state of directly realizing emptiness, itself is the antidote to the one hundred and twelve delusions. What is a direct antidote? A direct antidote is one that destroys something in the form of making it impossible for that something to return in the subsequent moment once the total destruction or eradication has been completed—in other words, one that eradicates something by bringing a permanent cessation in the place of the one that has been eradicated. Permanent cessation is nothing other than the mere factor of impossibility of the one hundred and twelve delusions returning once they have been eradicated.

Where does the cessation of the one hundred and twelve delusions take place? It takes place within the uninterrupted continuation of the meditative equipoise. In other words, the subsequent moment of the uninterrupted meditative equipoise that has eliminated the one hundred and twelve delusions is the same meditative equipoise in which the cessation of the one hundred and twelve delusions has taken place.

Very Joyous—The First Bhumi

At this stage, four accomplishments are all completed simultaneously: 1) the attainment of the direct realization of emptiness, 2) the total eradication of all one hundred and twelve acquired/learned afflictive delusions, 3) the achievement of reaching the first Bhumi, and 4) the perfection of giving. They are all achieved within one single sitting session by the meditator who has shifted from the fourth level of the Path of Preparation to the Path of Seeing

The perfection of giving is the first of the paramitas or perfections that constitute the advanced Mahayana Bodhisattva path. The perfection of giving is fully completed on the Path of Seeing so that the meditator not only engages in giving of whatever others ask for—even his or her own body—but also the thought and joy of giving arise even in his or her dreams.

The meditator is filled with much joy at giving his or her body to other sentient beings and this giving is free of any physical or mental pain. All the possibilities of physical and mental pain are numbed or overwhelmed by the force of the great joy that arises from giving his or her body for the purpose of others' needs and fulfillment. This is why Nagarjuna said in his *Ratnavali (Precious Garland)*: "How can one have mental pain from cutting one's body when one does not experience any physical pain?" Nagarjuna was pointing out that the perfection of giving is the unique spiritual accomplishment that is attained by someone on the first Bhumi.

There are three types of giving, all of which are accomplished when the meditator has attained the perfection of giving. They are: 1) giving material help, 2) giving protection from fear, and 3) giving Dharma teachings or teaching any wholesome skill that is useful for the recipient's worldly occupation.

On the third Path, the Path of Seeing, the meditator has fully eliminated the seeds of samsaric rebirth, and he or she is not subject to karmic rebirth. Regardless, he or she voluntarily takes rebirth in the samsaric realm under the influence of both compassion and the wishful prayer that is being made to dedicate his or her successive lives to the service of others' needs and fulfillment. The meditator's qualities of Bodhicitta and compassion have been realized previously and have increased during the maturation of the experience of emptiness.

After that, the meditator comes out of meditative equipoise and the conventional appearance soon returns to his or her perception. This whole event of coming out of meditative equipoise and the return of the conventional appearance to his or her perception is a state that is called the "post meditative state."

However, between coming out of meditative equipoise and the return of the conventional appearance to his or her perception—the "post meditative state— there is a brief state that is called the "subsequent non meditative state." It is also referred to as the "subsequent attainment." The period of the "subsequent non meditative state" is a brief moment in which the practitioner maintains the pure awareness of the illusory nature of conventional reality before entering the "post meditative state." In the non meditative period directly subsequent to meditative equipoise you have the full force or ability to interact with conventional reality, yet your perception is not being corrupted by the deceptive appearance of things and objects.

From the Path of Seeing onward, there is no need to improve the quality of the subjective ascertainment of emptiness no matter how much you meditate on it. However, there is still very much of a need to improve the quality of finding comfort in resting in emptiness during the meditation period, as well as finding comfort with your relation and interaction with the conventional world during the post meditative period. Although the actual mode of ascertainment of emptiness is completed on the Path of Seeing, your emotional comfort and familiarity with relating your life experience, interaction, and relations with the conventional world through the awareness of emptiness is not yet complete.

Path of Meditation and Remaining Nine Bhumis

As I said, the fourth Path, the Path of Meditation, has nine Bhumis. The Bhumis are attained in nine non dual meditative sitting sessions. Between each of these is a post meditative period. The practitioner might spend a long time in each post meditative period working towards the accumulation of merit.

It is very important to fully understand the distinction between the subsequent non meditative period and the post meditative period—both of which follow meditation. During the subsequent non meditative period, the practitioner, immediately upon arising from meditation, has a perception that is not yet corrupted by the deceptive appearances of conventional reality. The moment the meditator's perception returns to the corrupted, deceptive appearances of conventional reality up to the point where she or he re-enters the state of meditative equipoise is said to be the post meditative period. Just as the meditator can pass a long time in the post meditative period, he can also spend a long time in the subsequent non meditative state before he or she enters the period of the post meditative state. One can dwell for a long time in the subsequent non meditative state—seeing conventional reality as empty—and then lose that perception and be in the post meditative period/state. There is no fixed time for these periods to last because it depends on the individual.

The Path of Meditation has two levels of obstruction to be eliminated: 1) the obstruction of the "innate delusions" (the obstruction to Liberation) and 2) the cognitive obstruction to omniscience or Enlightenment. In the second through the seventh Bhumis, the practitioner is working toward the elimination of the obstruction of the "innate delusions."

The obstruction to omniscience is as mentioned previously a "cognitive flaw." In the eighth through the tenth Bhumis, the practitioner is working toward the elimination of this cognitive obstruction to Enlightenment. The cognitive flaw as the obstruction to omniscience is the extremely subtle potency or latency or imprint left in the cognitive mindstream by the misperception of all things and phenomena as inherently existent. On the Path of Meditation that latency can no longer become active in terms of turning into delusive thoughts and emotions and misperception.

To use an analogy: Say you keep garlic in a jar for a long time. After you use up all the garlic, the jar still has a smell of garlic that remains for days and days. That extremely subtle imprint—that cognitive flaw as the obstruction to omniscience—will never become active as a misperception of reality, just as the residual smell of the garlic will never become actual garlic.

The meditator who has achieved the first Bhumi (on the Path of Seeing) and is in the subsequent non meditative period belonging to the Path of Seeing enters the Fourth Path, the Path of Meditation, where he re-enters meditative equipoise, which serves as a direct antidote to the grossest part of the obscuration that is to be eliminated on the Path of Meditation. Once this has taken place the meditator is said to have reached the second Bhumi, Stainless.

The obscuration or obstruction of the innate delusions that is eliminated on the path of Meditation originated from the instinctual grasping at self. An instinctual grasping at self is a sense of an inherently existent "I," that is at the core of your being, not something taught and learned. This sense of "I," that is at the core of your being, does not require any temporary physical, emotional, or conceptual idea as a base in order to become active. Your false impression of the inherently existent "I" as an individual separate from other individuals always gets involved and interferes with your life experience and interaction with the world, whereas a sense of "I" as an American or as a Tibetan and the like requires a physical, emotional, or conceptual idea as a base in order to become active and interfere with your interaction with the world. A concept of nationality is a taught and learned sense of "I" based on ideas. The sense of "I" as a member of a particular group doesn't exist in every sentient being's mindstream from the beginning, from birth. The afflictive emotions arising from the instinctual or innate grasping at self are far subtler than the afflictive emotions arising from the conceptual or learned grasping at self.

The obstruction of the innate delusions has three levels of subtlety that are themselves further subdivided. All of these levels of subtlety are fully elaborated in the classical texts. So as not to confuse the less advanced reader, I simplify here in this presentation. The distinctions among the levels of obstruction lie in their subtleties, which means how easily they can be eliminated. Each one of the Bhumis eliminates or removes its respective object of elimination by bringing a permanent cessation in the place of what is being eliminated.

The way each of the nine Bhumis eliminates its respective object of elimination by its own force is a bit like repeatedly washing a dirty shirt by getting rid of the dirt collected on it. You get rid of the dirt on the shirt from the most gross to the most subtle by rubbing or scraping it nine times. Each effort of rubbing or scraping removes the corresponding dirt that needs to be removed. Each time you wash the shirt, it gets cleaner, as the dirt that has collected on it becomes fainter and fainter, less and less.

Stainless—The Second Bhumi

As said before, on the third Path, the Path of Seeing, the meditator eliminates the one hundred and twelve acquired/learned afflictive delusions at the first Bhumi, called Very Joyous. Then he or she passes onto the fourth Path, the Path of Meditation, where the later moment or instant of meditative equipoise—the non dualistic direct experience of emptiness where and in which relative or conventional reality ceases to appear and emptiness is left—is very lucid. The meditator's mind is more like inseparably infused with emptiness.

It is here that this very lucid experience of emptiness serves as a direct antidote to the grossest portion or level of the obscuration of innate delusions to be eliminated on the Path of Meditation, and this belongs to the second Bhumi, Stainless. Progressively the view of emptiness is strengthening and the delusion of the inherent existence of phenomena is weakening. The meditator moves from the first Bhumi to the second Bhumi, through meditative state to meditative state, uninterrupted by a post meditative period. Between each succeeding Bhumi, however, there is a post meditation period.

Right after the first Bhumi, 1) the attainment of the second Bhumi, as well as 2) the total elimination of the most gross part of the obscuration of the innate delusions to be eliminated on the Path of Meditation, and 3) the perfection of ethics are all three completed simultaneously.

The perfection of ethics is fully completed at this stage and the meditator will not have any unwholesome thoughts even in his or her dreams. There are three types of ethics. The first one entails the ethics of abstention from negative actions of body, speech, and mind. Negative action is any action, behavior, or lifestyle that has a natural potential to create disharmony in your relationships and interaction with the world. Such negative actions are killing, stealing, sexual misconduct, lying, divisive speech, insulting speech, idle gossip, covetousness, ill will, and biased attitudes with roots of wrong reason. The second type of ethics entails collecting or accumulating virtuous deeds or merit. The third type entails the ethics of benefiting sentient beings for their temporary and ultimate needs.

Luminous—The Third Bhumi

On this stage, the meditator simultaneously 1) eliminates another level of subtlety in the obscuration (innate delusions) and 2) accomplishes the perfection of patience.

Patience is an extremely important element in spiritual practice. The essence of the Buddha's teachings and its practice is to abandon harming others and to give help, neither of which is possible without the practice of patience. If you are tempted to respond with anger to another's hostility and harm, you still have the impulse to cause harm to others. And therefore you have not realized the Buddha's teaching that one must train to be harmless to others in thought, word, and deed.

In *Lama Cho-Pa*, the text in the tantric tradition of Guru Yoga practice written by the second Panchen Lama, who was the second most high ranking reincarnated lama of Tibet, the importance of patience is emphasized in this way:

> Should even the myriad of beings of the three realms of existence without exception,
> Become angry at me, criticize, humiliate, blame, falsely accuse, even threaten to kill me,
> I seek your (Guru's) blessing to practice the perfection of patience,
> And to work for their benefit in response to their harm (done to me).

Patience is an act of remaining calm in the face of others' harm and hostility without responding with anger, frustration, and annoyance. On the third Bhumi, the subtlest residual impulse from which you might do harm to others is completely eradicated. Therefore, the perfection of patience is completed.

There are three types of patience: the patience of not retaliating to those who have caused harm or injury; the patience of voluntarily accepting hardship; and the patience of gaining certainty with regard to the teachings and to practice.

The first type of patience is an antidote to animosity. The second type of patience is an antidote to discouragement and disheartenment, and the third type of patience is an antidote to doubt in the teachings along with any reluctance to engage in the practice. You are not a true practitioner if you don't see spiritual meaning and value in the practice of patience. Patience is surely not a sign of weakness. Rather it is a sign of nobility and of greatness of being.

Radiant—The Fourth Bhumi

On this stage, the meditator simultaneously 1) eliminates another level of subtlety of the obscuration of the innate delusions and 2) accomplishes the perfection of enthusiastic effort (diligence, joyous effort).

Enthusiastic effort is joyous or joyful effort in doing wholesome activities. It is an antidote to laziness, an antidote to the inclination to easiness. Laziness gives rise to stress, weariness and frustration arising from the unrealistic expectation about what you are striving for. Laziness prevents you from finding pleasure and comfort in the cultivation of the cause for what you are striving to gain or reach. You then are irritated by not achieving it within the time period that you had expected. If this is the case, then you are not living with the cultivation of the cause but you are living with your desire for the result of the cause that you are not cultivating owing to laziness, which makes you irritated each time you sit and practice.

The lack of joyful effort in your Dharma practice seriously delays your attainment of Enlightenment by causing you to relapse into worldly distractions and time consuming meaningless delusional activities.

There are three types of enthusiastic effort: armor-like enthusiastic effort, enthusiastic effort in the performance of virtuous activities, and enthusiastic effort in working for the welfare of sentient beings.

Armor-like enthusiastic effort is full preparedness to perform by every means possible to accomplish your objective no matter how long it takes, and how much you face hardship and difficulties. None of those can prevent you from achieving your ultimate objective, and your will and inner strength cannot be shaken by hardships and difficulties that you might face on the cultivation of the Path.

Enthusiastic effort in the performance of virtuous activity is a delight in the practice of the perfections as well as in other unselfish activities. Enthusiastic effort in working for the welfare of sentient beings is wholeheartedly dedicating your physical energy and resources to helping them and joyfully seeking an opportunity to help according to their needs and inclinations, rather than helping them due to what you believe you have to offer or what you think their real needs are. Failing to help others according to their real needs and inclinations will often turn your help into harm. This really causes your good motivation and unselfish effort to be ineffective.

Difficult to Overcome—The Fifth Bhumi

On this stage the meditator simultaneously 1) eliminates yet another level of subtlety of the obscuration of innate delusions and 2) accomplishes the perfection of concentration or single pointedness.

Since the perfection of concentration is attained at this fifth Bhumi, the meditator's mind will remain in a calm and undistracted state even in the post meditation period. He or she henceforth will not have any mind-distracting conceptual or emotional responses to sense stimuli even if there is a full interaction between the five senses and their usual objects of form, sound, smell, taste, and touch. The subtle tendency of conceptual and emotional responses to arise from sense stimuli is completely eradicated upon reaching the fifth Bhumi. The meditator's mind will never associate with delusions. The risk of his or her mind coming under the spell of delusion is removed forever.

For an ordinary being, the conceptual and emotional responses to sense stimuli are inevitable, and as a result the mind is naturally disturbed and distracted. Up until the fifth Bhumi, the instinctual tendencies for attraction to sense stimuli are always present in the post meditative period even for those who have attained true Shamatha and the fourth Bhumi.

Approaching—The Sixth Bhumi

On this stage, the meditator simultaneously 1) eliminates another subtlety of the obstruction of innate delusions to be eliminated on the Path of Meditation and 2) accomplishes the perfection of wisdom. The perfection of wisdom refers to the wisdom realizing the emptiness of all phenomena. Until now the meditator has been at each stage becoming more and more familiar with the wisdom realizing emptiness, but here at the sixth Bhumi that wisdom realizing emptiness finally becomes mature. Since the wisdom realizing emptiness is perfected, nothing can serve as a condition to give rise to a thought of objects or things being inherently existent. Total freedom from grasping and clinging onto things on the basis of their false appearance of being inherently existent has taken place on this, the sixth Bhumi.

A profound awareness of emptiness and the experience of realizing that objects are not what they appear to be are spontaneously present. The meditator is now fully capable of living continuously within the felt presence of the ultimate truth of the emptiness of all phenomena. All method aspects of practice are now perfectly clarified because the meditator has now gained a clear sight of reality and he or she cultivates the method aspects within the realization, the continuously felt presence of the truth of emptiness.

The speed of spiritual progress is now much stronger and faster than ever before. However, the meditator's capability to live according to what things and objects really are is slightly delayed by the remnant force of the false appearance. The meditator knows full well that the appearance of things as if they are inherently real is false, but this still persisting remnant force of false appearance will never cause the meditator to believe in the way things appear. Things might still appear to the meditator as if they are inherently real, but he or she knows with confidence that this appearance is false. To repeat, the still persisting remnant force of false appearance will never cause the meditator to believe in the way things appear.

The experience of seeing the false appearance is similar to seeing the false appearance of a coiled rope as a snake. When the coiled rope appears to your mind as a snake, it appears to your mind as being that which is not what it actually is. A coiled rope appearing as a snake is, in reality, what is out there, and there is a slight delay until you realize that what you first thought was a snake is only a coiled rope.

What should appear out there on the ground in reality is just a harmless coiled rope, but what appears to your mind is a harmful snake, not a harmless rope. This mistaken appearance puts you in the same feeling of danger as a snake would, but in conventional reality the snake is not out there threatening you.

A person who knows that the coiled rope is not a snake and who has no room to believe in it as a snake can have an initial false impression of the rope being a snake. The false appearance, which causes the impression of the rope being a snake, will cause a time gap wherein it is impossible for the perceiver to be able to live according to the fact that the rope is just a rope. However, such a person will not act upon the false appearance of the rope being a snake, due to the active presence of his or her awareness of the rope not being a snake.

In brief, the false appearance of the rope being a snake cannot evoke an emotion of fear, panic, or anger in the mind of a person who clearly knows that it is not a snake even if it appears as a snake.

A meditator who has reached the sixth Bhumi cannot have a thought that things and objects exist inherently, and thus never experiences an emotional reaction to the false appearance of things and objects appearing to be what they are not. The false appearance, in this case, is the appearance of things and objects as being something more than a mere name, something that is findable at their material or physical level. This is how things normally appear to your naive perception—as more than a mere name, as more than what they are. However, things and objects do not exist as something more than a mere name, and therefore they cannot be found at their material or physical level under ultimate analysis.

Not finding the things and objects to be what you normally thought them to be under careful analysis is not proof that they are nonexistent. It is merely proof that they do not exist in the way they normally appear to your naive perception.

It is important to make a distinction between "not having found" and "having found the nonexistence" of something. Merely not having found the inherent existence of the table is not the meaning of having found the nonexistence of the inherently existent table-ness.

Merely not having found the inherent existence of the table alone cannot dispel the wrong notion of the inherent existence of the table. That is, you still may hold the notion that somehow the table exists inherently but you have just not been able to reach or fully confirm it yet. In contrast, when you have found the nonexistence of inherently existing table-ness, this understanding fully dispels the wrong notion of the inherent existence of the table. The mind grasping at the inherent existence of the table is now disqualified or eliminated.

For example, you lose a tiny needle somewhere in your house and search for it, but come up with a negative result of not having found that lost needle. Merely not having found the lost needle alone is not the meaning of having found the nonexistence of the needle. The reason for this is because merely not having found—failing to find—the lost needle alone cannot dispel the idea or conviction that the needle exists somewhere in the house. The need to search for it still remains within you and you still have the hope of finding it. That is why you must find the nonexistence of the needle to be able to quit hoping that you will find it.

Having found the nonexistence of the needle dispels the doubt and the need to search for it ceases permanently. The cessation of the need to search for the lost needle brings you permanent rest from wanting to search for it.

Merely not having found the lost needle is nothing more than not seeing the needle, which is very different from seeing the nonexistence of the needle. Similarly, merely not having found the inherent existence of the table is not the meaning of having found the nonexistence of the inherent existence of the table. Evidence of the absence of the inherent existence of the table is the emptiness of the table, and it is much more than not having found the inherent existence of the table. Having found the nonexistence of the inherent existence of the table is actually having found the evidence of the lack of inherent existence, and it is much more than merely not having found the evidence of inherent existence. In brief, the lack of evidence is not the meaning of evidence of the lack.

Emptiness is the lack of inherent existence, whereas the lack of evidence of the inherent existence is merely not having found it (inherent existence), merely not having found what you were looking for.

So, when you realize emptiness you must have found something, a very fresh phenomenon, within the context of not having found what you are searching for. For example, when you are searching for the inherent existence of the table through the application of ultimate analysis and come up with a negative result of not having found it, merely not having found the inherent existence of the table is not the meaning of having found the emptiness of the table unless you have found the evidence of its lack. The evidence of the lack of inherent existence of the table is the emptiness of the table. Therefore, when you realize the emptiness of the table, you must have found a very fresh phenomenon in the place of not having found what you are searching for.

What you are searching for through ultimate analysis is the inherent existence of the table. You must disprove the possibility of inherent existence by applying ultimate analysis as described above. You will find the emptiness of the object as something fresh to be tasted or experienced, instead of merely not finding the inherent existence of the object table.

As I said, the perfection of wisdom is accomplished on the sixth Bhumi. There are three types of wisdom: 1) the wisdom realizing conventional phenomena without contradicting their ultimate nature of being empty; 2) the wisdom realizing ultimate phenomena without that realization giving rise to a conflict of why things appear solid and existent in and of themselves as opposed to them being empty of independent and inherent existence; 3) the wisdom realizing the skillful means of working for the welfare of sentient beings whose inclinations, predispositions, attitudes, behaviors and needs are so different and complex.

In brief, wisdom is like an eye that sees things clearly, as they are. When you have realized the three types of wisdom, you don't have to imagine what all phenomena are when you see them. An ordinary mind sees things no differently than the imagination. In other words, your ordinary mind sees only what you think. It does not see what is out there to be seen in reality. Not seeing what is out there to see, and instead seeing what you think is out there, indicates that you are seeing nothing other than your own imagination.

Gone Afar—The Seventh Bhumi

On this stage, the meditator simultaneously 1) eliminates the final subtleties of the obstruction (the innate delusions) to liberation that is to be eliminated on the Path of Meditation, and 2) accomplishes the perfection of skillful means.

Skillful means is the capability to act in accordance with the inclinations, predispositions and needs of other sentient beings. Skillful means is using every action either as a direct cause to give relief and comfort, or as an indirect cause for others to gain liberation by bringing them to the Dharmic life.

In brief, skillful means is wisdom that is pregnant with great compassion and working for the welfare of sentient beings whose inclinations, predispositions, attitudes, behaviors and needs are all very different and complex. Every single act of helping, stemming from this wisdom, effectively fulfills and meets the real needs and inclinations of sentient beings.

The meditator who has reached the seventh Bhumi is fully capable of helping others according to their real needs and inclinations rather than helping in a way that he or she thinks they need help. The reason why much of your ordinary help goes wrong is that you are not helping according to others' real needs and inclinations. Rather you are helping according to what you think their real needs are. This problem has been fully overcome when you accomplish the perfection of skillful means upon reaching the seventh Bhumi called Gone Afar.

Immovable—The Eighth Bhumi

On this stage, the meditator begins to eliminate the cognitive flaw or obstruction to Enlightenment or omniscience. This cognitive obstruction has three levels of subtlety: small-large, small-medium, and small-small.

With the seventh Bhumi the meditator has gained the full cessation or liberation or Nirvana, by the permanent eradication of the obstruction to liberation (the innate delusions), and he or she may remain in meditative absorption in that cessation for a long period of time, forgetting to continue working on eliminating the obstruction to omniscience.

If the meditator has gotten lost in meditation after the seventh Bhumi, an enlightened being or Buddha finally wakes him or her from meditative absorption in cessation by sending a telepathic message: "Oh my son/daughter! Wake up and return to post meditation to work on eliminating the obstruction to omniscience in order to achieve the non dual blissful awareness of the ultimate truth of emptiness simultaneously with the conventional truth of deceptive appearance."

Upon heeding the exhortation of the enlightened being and waking from the meditative absorption in cessation or Nirvana, the meditator 1) eliminates the gross or large part of the obstruction to omniscience during the last part of the eighth Bhumi, and at the same time 2) accomplishes the perfection of aspirational prayer.

The aspirational prayer is an earthshaking compassionate wish with the willpower to carry the meaning of the prayer in action as long as the need is there. Actually, from then on every single positive action of body, speech and mind is prayer.

Acharya Shantideva made the following aspirational prayer in his *Guide to the Bodhisattva's Way of Life*:

> As long as space remains,
>
> As long as sentient beings remain,
>
> Until then, may I too remain,
>
> To dispel the miseries of the world.

The most subtle residual tendency to have reluctance to carry out the meaning of the words, promises, prayers and wishes in actual action whenever the need is there is fully eradicated upon reaching the eighth Bhumi called Immovable.

Excellence—The Ninth Bhumi

At this stage, the meditator 1) eliminates the middling part of the obstruction to omniscience, and 2) accomplishes the perfection of power.

The perfection of power is a mental power that, without any intentional thought, one performs as an instantaneous activity to help others (who are karmically and mentally ripened) at the exact time when help is needed. It is an instantaneous response to others' call for help without any discrimination from your side. The others' call for help ignites an action within you without any intentional thought from your side.

Just as a defective seed cannot be affected by rainwater and will never germinate, similarly, beings with an immature mind cannot be affected by the enlightened shower of Dharma. However, those beings who are already mentally and karmically ripened are affected by the instantaneously offered beneficial activities whose performances have been perfected by those who have reached the ninth Bhumi called Excellence.

Cloud of Dharma—The Tenth Bhumi

At this stage, the meditator 1) eliminates the final and subtlest part of the obstruction to Enlightenment, and 2) accomplishes the perfection of primordial wisdom.

The perfection of primordial wisdom is different from the perfection of wisdom realizing emptiness, which has been perfected at the sixth Bhumi. Primordial wisdom is the mind's natural quality of being able to perceive all conventional phenomena free from duality, in the same way as perceiving the ultimate nature of all phenomena as empty, free from duality. Until the perfection of primordial wisdom, the ultimate phenomena of emptiness and the conventional phenomena of appearance have not yet become simultaneous objects of a single moment of non conceptual awareness.

In the very last moment of the perfection of primordial wisdom upon reaching the tenth Bhumi, the meditator's mind turns into an omniscient consciousness and has reached the Path of No More Learning or "beyond training."

Path of No More Learning

The fifth Path, the Path of No More Learning, is the non dual blissful awareness of an omniscient mind that is characterized by the perfection of abandonment and the perfection of attainment. It is the permanent unification of meditative and post meditative awareness perceiving simultaneously the two truths—the ultimate truth of emptiness and the conventional truth of appearance.

This is the highest form of spiritual attainment that can be achieved and it can be achieved by every human being.

The term that Buddhists use for such spiritual realization is Buddhahood, which means Enlightenment. Enlightenment is an all knowing, blissful state of mind and a blissful state of being where there is no more increase and there is no more decrease. It is the purest state of mind in which there is nothing left to be purified and nothing left to be realized. It is fully blossomed, fully awakened, and beyond training.

The Three Kayas

In the moment the practitioner attains Enlightenment, at the last moment of the tenth Bhumi, he does not disappear but maintains psychophysical existence. That is, he continues to maintain the physical body and internal realization and attainment in the fully perfected state, with no increase and no decrease. If there would be increase it would mean that there was something still more to move on to, but there is nothing left to move on to, nothing farther or higher to be attained. If there would be decrease, it would mean that there was room for relapsing or falling back or that the enlightened one would be subject to lose his or her perfected state.

The three Kayas are the final results of the elimination of 1) the obstruction to Enlightenment, 2) the full completion of accumulation of merit, and 3) the meditative equipoise on emptiness reaching its highest peak.

The three Kayas are Dharmakaya, Nirmanakaya, and Sambhogakaya. The practitioner attains the three Kayas as his or her enlightened features simultaneously upon the elimination of the subtlest obstruction to Enlightenment at the last moment of the tenth Bhumi. The idea of three Kayas is unique to Mahayana Buddhism. Kaya means form or body.

The first kaya is called Dharmakaya, which means "truth body," the highest level of blissful supreme wisdom that retains the cessation of permanent elimination of the two obstructions (the obstruction to Nirvana and the obstruction to Enlightenment) as described above.

The second kaya is called Nirmanakaya, which means "emanation body." It is originated or manifested from the Sambhogakaya (see below) in order to perform enlightened activities in the ordinary world through a gross physical form, which can be perceived by ordinary beings and have interaction with them.

The third kaya is called Sambhogakaya, which means "enjoyment body," which is the highest attainment within the sphere of matter, but is the most subtle form of an enlightened being who is inseparably one with the highest state of bliss and who is not perceptible to ordinary beings.

The Sakyamuni Buddha is said to be the Nirmanakaya and therefore is accessible to ordinary sentient beings so that they may receive Dharma teaching through various means in accordance to their karmic background, quantity of collection of merit, and level of perceptual advancement.

Conclusions

1. The true search for Enlightenment should begin with the cultivation of proper ethical discipline as a foundation. This means mindfully refraining from the ten negative actions and joyfully cultivating the ten positive actions that reach beyond merely not doing negative or harmful things.

2. One must seriously engage in and practice purification of negativity, karmic obstructions and other psychic mildew to make the foundation free from inner obstacles for the proper spiritual growth.

    The most effective purification practices are 1) the Vajrasattva purification practice involving the mindful recitation of the hundred seed syllable Vajrasattva mantra, and 2) the recitation of the names of the thirty-five purification Buddhas along with prostration.

3. One also needs to seriously engage in the practice of the accumulation of merit, or *punya* in Sanskrit. Merit is positive spiritual energy that serves as fertilizer making the foundation soil of ethical discipline and intellectual understanding (of emptiness, and subtle impermanence, for example) fertile, rich, and stable enough for your practice to progress quickly. Though there are many ways you can accumulate merit, the mandala offering and rejoicing in the virtuous deeds of yourself and others are the most effective and powerful.

4. You must make sure you have a complete understanding of the general structure of the Buddhist Paths and Bhumis in their sequential order as well, because an understanding of these Paths and Bhumis is a necessary condition for their perfection. Therefore, it is extremely important to find a qualified teacher who can teach you from his or her inner personal experience rather than giving you superficial dry knowledge or information.

    You can receive teaching from different teachers and from different lineages. However, it is important to stick with one teacher and his quintessential instructions when it comes down to the actual practice.

    Your root Guru should be the one from whom you have received major teachings, initiations, transmissions, precepts, refuge, and quintessential instructions on how to go about the paths of Buddhist practice flawlessly.

5. It is very important not to accept the teachings out of blind faith or without testing them. You must put the teachings to a real test and do thorough experimentation by applying various analyses until you personally find the truth of them and gain full conviction.

6. Also it is extremely important to combine three things: intellectual study, contemplation or reflective thinking, and meditation. It is these that are needed in order to digest the conceptual and intellectual concepts. It is certain that you will get sick if the information you receive by listening to the teachings is not properly digested through contemplation and meditation. For example, you may get sick when the food in your stomach is not digested properly before you eat your second meal.

    Nothing can go into your spiritual system if you don't emphasize reflective thinking on teaching topics and meditating on them with non conceptual awareness. If you simply focus on intellectual study by listening to teachings it will not take you beyond mere information.

You cannot attain this vital non conceptual awareness simply by reading books and listening to teachings. To have this experience you must pass from one state of awareness to another, moving gradually to deeper and deeper levels of non conceptual awareness. In meditation this is exactly what happens: in sequential order, you pass from one level of awareness to the next level of awareness of the ultimate truth of reality.

Studying and listening to the teachings are extremely important, just as important as contemplation and meditation. But conceptual and intellectual understanding gained from listening to teaching remains like the rock that is always dry inside although it sits at the bottom of the ocean for eons.

7   You must embark on serious meditation practice aiming at bringing a real long-lasting mind transformation, step by step, until you attain Enlightenment. The way you travel toward the realization of Enlightenment is by training on the five Paths and ten Bhumis as explained above.

The progress you will make on the five Paths and ten Bhumis is very slow and gradual, but you are getting closer to the attainment of Enlightenment each time you sit in meditation. Perfecting the earlier stages of the Path is a necessary condition in order to move into the later stages of the Path.

The cultivation of the actual Paths and Bhumis requires that you periodically limit physical, vocal, and mental activity in isolation from your daily ordinary activity and interaction with the rest of the world. This isolation can be done by going into strict retreat at least two times a year aiming to practice and accomplish certain aspects of the Path, which you cannot do in your daily practice done while carrying on with your ordinary

8\. You must know that 1) renunciation (the definite decision to be free of samsara), 2) Bodhicitta (the aspiration to attain Enlightenment for the benefit of all sentient beings), and 3) the flawless view of emptiness (discussed in detail in chapters six and seven) are fundamental ingredients of your spiritual practice. They must be present in every part of your practice—without these three no realization can arise, no matter how long you practice or have been practicing.

It is said that renunciation is the gateway to Nirvana and that Bodhicitta is the gateway to non abiding Nirvana or Enlightenment. The flawless view of emptiness is the one that takes you either to a Nirvanic state or to an enlightened state through one of the two gateways.

9\. Dharma means "that which changes your mind," or "that which brings inner mind transformation and spiritual evolution by cutting the causal process of karmic degeneration."

Your Dharma practice must serve as an antidote to your delusions, helping to increase the awareness of mind, making you less dependent upon external circumstances for your happiness, and making you more capable to be a mindful, compassionate, and concerned person toward others' welfare before making any decision to do anything in your daily life.

Changing external physical religious aspects is easy and not of much use or meaning. Changing your inner mind and thoughts, and cultivating mental religious qualities is very difficult and really takes time. You should be persistent and determined and be a joyful practitioner rather than a frustrated practitioner who is disheartened at not attaining something within your own expected time period.

10

The Guru is the root of all perfections and realizations, and is the source of blessings and transmission, as stated by Lama Tsong-Khapa. It is extremely important to maintain a healthy, spiritual relationship with your Guru by keeping your perception clean and pure towards the Guru.

Guru is a Sanskrit word, which means spiritual teacher. The word guru is composed of two syllables. The syllable "gu" means "darkness" and the syllable "ru" means "light."

A true Guru dispels the disciple's ignorance and bestows light. He takes away the disciple's wrong understanding, wrong belief, and his delusional imperfections, and grants him the highest light of wisdom.

The meaning or definition of Guru in the Tibetan Buddhist tradition is "one who has deep spiritual experience and wisdom knowledge that has nothing above it."

To have a Guru is not just important but necessary in your pursuit of Dharma and your search for higher spiritual realization. And also it is necessary to realize that the teachings and instructions are as a nectar-like panacea for your delusional imperfections and samsaric existence where there are no long lasting peace and happiness. Not only are there no long lasting peace and happiness but even the momentary pleasure also turns into a cause for long lasting pain and suffering.

You must work hard to realize that your Guru is the Buddha, and that his teachings and instructions are as nectar. Without realizing this, you cannot attain spiritual realization in any circumstance.

About the Author

GESHE DAKPA TOPGYAL is well known for his particularly skillful means in presenting Tibetan Buddhism to the Western mind in its culture. In addition to his years of experience and expertise, Geshe-la brings a kind heart and a sense of humor to his teaching that is both disarming and endearing.

He was born in the Western region of Tibet, but fled to India at the age of six. He entered Drepung Loseling Monastery at the age of ten and received his Geshe degree (Doctorate of Religion and Philosophy) twenty-two years later in 1992.

He taught for many years in Europe before coming to the United States. Between 1993 and 1994, he visited one hundred and twenty American cities giving lectures on Tibetan Buddhism and culture, and led a number of meditation retreats.

Currently, he teaches students year round and serves as spiritual director of the Charleston Tibetan Society Dharma Center as well as the South Carolina Dharma Group in Columbia, South Carolina.

In addition to the books listed in the front of this text, Geshe Topgyal has published practice manuals on topics such as Shamatha meditation, Vajrasattva purification, Guru Yoga of Lama Tsong-Khapa, Manjushri Sadhana Practice, Tara Sadhana Practice, Medicine Buddha Healing Practice, and Chenrezig Meditation and Mental Recitation of the Sacred Mantra of Chenrezig.

www.ingramcontent.com/pod-product-compliance
Lightning Source LLC
Chambersburg PA
CBHW072015110526
44592CB00012B/1317